In a decade and a half in Japan, **Rob Goss** has visited almost every corner of the country—from Hokkaido in the north to Okinawa in the sub-tropical south—in the process writing about Japan for magazines such as Time, National Geographic Traveler and almost 100 other publications around the globe. Of all the places Rob has visited, nowhere draws him back as often or effortlessly as Japan's captivating former capitals, Kyoto and Nara. The pockets of tranquility and tradition that permeate these cities create an enchanting contrast to Tokyo, where Rob lives, providing rich and varied subject matter for a writer. As any regular visitor will tell you, on each visit Kyoto and Nara gradually reveal a little more of their magic. Each time, you fall a little deeper under their spell. Rob is the author of three other books published by Tuttle: the award-winning *Tuttle Travel Pack: Japan*, which won a Gold Award from the North American Travel Journalists Association, *Tuttle Travel Pack: Tokyo* and the NATJA Silver Award-winning *Tokyo: Capital of Cool*.

Published by Tuttle Publishing, an imprint of Periplus Editions (HK) Ltd

www.tuttlepublishing.com

Copyright © 2016 Periplus Editions (HK) Ltd
(Refer to Photo Credits page for photos ©)

ISBN: 978-4-8053-1179-0

Distributed by

North America, Latin America & Europe
Tuttle Publishing
364 Innovation Drive
North Clarendon, VT 05759-9436 U.S.A.
Tel: 1 (802) 773-8930
Fax: 1 (802) 773-6993
info@tuttlepublishing.com
www.tuttlepublishing.com

Japan
Tuttle Publishing
Yaekari Building, 3rd Floor
5-4-12 Osaki, Shinagawa-ku
Tokyo 141-0032
Tel: (81) 3 5437-0171
Fax: (81) 3 5437-0755
sales@tuttle.co.jp
www.tuttle.co.jp

Asia Pacific
Berkeley Books Pte. Ltd.
61 Tai Seng Avenue, #02-12
Singapore 534167
Tel: (65) 6280-1330
Fax: (65) 6280-6290
inquiries@periplus.com.sg
www.periplus.com

18 17 16   10 9 8 7 6 5 4 3 2 1

Printed in China   1605CM

TUTTLE TRAVEL PACK

KYOTO
AND NARA

GUIDE
+ MAP

Rob Goss

TUTTLE Publishing

Tokyo | Rutland, Vermont | Singapore

DISCOVERING KYOTO'S ELUSIVE SOUL

Let's start with something of a confession: it took me a few years of living in Japan before I "got" Kyoto and Nara. Initially coming to Tokyo after university to teach English for a year, I had very little interest in golden temples, *geisha* districts and ornately landscaped gardens. As for my take on foreigners who were into Kyoto and Nara, it seemed to me like they had all become more Japanese than the Japanese; wearing *kimono*, bowing on the phone and composing *haiku* under the cherry blossoms. All a bit weird.

Then I visited the cities. The way the gilded Kinkaku-ji in Kyoto cast its reflection into the pond before it had me snapping away on my camera like a madman. The colors and aromas of the food stalls along Nishiki-koji were addictive. The gardens of Tofuku-ji Temple were mesmerizing. Tokyo is a great city to call home, but by comparison Kyoto and Nara felt almost serene—calm and mature compared to the brashness and fickleness of Japan's capital. I've always thought that traditional Japan's soul and mine aren't really natural bedfellows. With Japan's ancient capitals, I guess, it's a case of opposites attracting.

Each time I return, it feels like I stumble on something new. On one trip while writing this book, it was a first visit to the ancient moss gardens of Saiho-ji—eerie and dank, and only accessible after copying out Japanese sutra at the temple. On another trip, I remember sitting on the wooden steps next to Ryoan-ji's famous dry landscape garden and noticing for the first time a weeping cherry blossom reaching over the garden's wall. The two cities hold so much history, mystery and allure that I don't think I'll ever grow tired of going back. I hope this book will help you discover some of that magic for yourself. Happy travels!

CONTENTS

Kyoto & Nara at a Glance

The city of Kyoto is situated in the center of Honshu, Japan's main island, about 370 kilometers (230 miles) west of Tokyo and 30 kilometers (20 miles) east of Osaka. The city, which is part of the wider Kyoto Prefecture, is comprised of eleven *ku* (wards) that are run by a single city council. The eleven wards, which are home to the vast majority of Kyoto's main sights, cover 828km² (320 mi²), while the entire Kyoto Prefecture stretches to 4,613 km² (1780mi²). Directly south is Nara Prefecture and within it the city of Nara, which is considerably smaller than Kyoto at just 276km² (105mi²). Just 40 km (25 miles) and an easy 45-minute train journey separate the two cities.

A Brief History

Nara served as Japan's capital from 710 to 784, while Kyoto was officially established as the country's capital, named Heian-kyo, in 794, although people had been living in the area for centuries prior. The first Aoi Matsuri (page 76) was held in what would become the city of Kyoto in 544, and before that the Hata clan had settled in what is now the Sagano district and laid early foundations for the city by developing flood control measures. From 794 through to 1868, when the Meiji Restoration saw the emperor and capital status move to Tokyo, Kyoto remained the home of the emperor and with it the country's capital. The only exception was the period 1192–1333, when under the Minamoto clan, power shifted to the Kamakura shogunate in Kamakura.

Unlike Tokyo and many other cities in Japan, Kyoto managed to avoid the worst ravages of World War Two. Much of it was, however, levelled during the bloody Onin War of 1467–77, the catalyst for Japan's turbulent 150 year-long Sengoku Jidai (Country at War period), which eventually culminated with the unification of Japan under the Tokugawa shogunate.

Kyotoites

At last count, Kyoto's population was roughly 1.5 million, making it the eighth largest city in Japan, behind (in order) Tokyo, Yokohama, Osaka, Nagoya, Sapporo, Kobe and Fukuoka. The population of the whole of Kyoto Prefecture is approximately 2.6 million. Like Japan as a whole, aside from the large numbers of foreign tourists who visit the city (some 500,000 a year), Kyoto has a very low number of non-Japanese residents. Nara almost feels like a town by comparison, with a population of approximately 370,000.

Language

Japanese is the first language of 99% of the Japanese population. With a complex

Gion district

Maiko in full dress

hotels, and many of the major tourist attractions. Many tourist attractions, shops and restaurants will have English signs, labels or menus prepared as well. All that said, it's worth learning a few basic phrases. The locals will certainly appreciate any effort you make, no matter how mangled. If you'd like to try, have a look at the section on useful expressions and pronunciation on page 90.

Religion

Most Japanese don't consider themselves to be religious—more than 80% say they have no religious affiliation and approximately 65% don't believe in God or Buddha. It's better to think of Buddhism, which arrived from China in the 6th century, and Shinto, the indigenous religion of Japan, forming one set of traditional practices that are followed by the majority. In fact, that's why the Japanese sometimes say they are born Shinto but die Buddhist, in reference to the traditional rituals used for birth and death. Shrines are Shinto, temples are Buddhist. Besides these two religions, between 1% and 2% of the population are Christian and a smaller number Muslim.

system of honorifics and three separate writing systems (the complicated *kanji* and less difficult, phonetic *hiragana* and *katakana*) that between them use thousands of different characters, it isn't an easy language to learn. Fortunately, even though Japan consistently ranks poorly among Asian countries for English proficiency levels, you will be able to enjoy Kyoto and Nara without knowing any Japanese—there will be someone who can speak English at tourist offices, most

Yasaka Shrine

HOW TO USE THIS BOOK

Tuttle Travel Pack Kyoto & Nara kicks off with a brief overview of Kyoto and Nara, taking a look at the two cities' history, people and more, then Chapter 1 covers Kyoto and Nara's 'Don't Miss' Sights, detailing the top 11 places to visit and things to do—from strolling the meditative grounds of Ginkaku-ji temple and contemplating the cryptic design of Ryoan-ji's Zen rock garden to exploring the bamboo grove in Arashiyama and enlivening the senses with a wander around Nishiki-koji food market.

In Chapter 2, we break Kyoto and Nara down into nine day-long and half day-long guides, one day starting at Kiyomizu Temple and the shop-filled lanes leading from it and ending at Chion-in Temple; other days taking in sights such as the gilded temple of Kinkaku-ji and the gardens of Daitoku-ji, or exploring the cluster of UNESCO World Heritage sites in Nara.

In Chapter 3: Author's Recommendations, our Japan-based author makes his picks for Kyoto and Nara's best hotels and restaurants, top kid-friendly attractions, best places to shop, best cultural experiences, must-see galleries and museums, and more. Lastly, the Travel Tips section presents all you need to know before you go, including the lowdown on visas, health and safety advice, important points of etiquette, transport, useful Japanese, and much more to help you enjoy Japan's captivating formal capitals with the minimum of fuss and worry.

While all information is correct at time of print, please do make sure to check ahead if you plan to visit any of the venues listed within, as hotels, shops and restaurants may close and every so often tourist attractions (especially historic) undergo major renovations. As such, the publisher cannot accept responsibility for any errors that may be contained within the Travel Pack.

CHAPTER 1
KYOTO & NARA'S
'Don't Miss' Sights

After more than 1,000 years as Japan's imperial capital, the Kyoto that greets modern-day visitors has numerous reminders of the city's rich history. The 11 'Don't Miss' sights here represent the most captivating of those remnants of both ancient Kyoto and the capital before it, Nara, from the decadent golden temple of Kinkaku-ji and the more reserved dry landscape garden at Ryoan-ji to the seemingly endless rows of red *torii* gateways at Fushimi Inari Shrine and ancient wooden structures at Horyu-ji Temple—the places that make Kyoto and Nara so unforgettable.

1   Kinkaku-ji, the Golden Pavilion
2   Ryoan-ji's Zen Rock Garden
3   Kiyomizu Temple
4   Nijo Castle
5   Fushimi Inari Shrine
6   The Gion District
7   Arashiyama's Bamboo Grove
8   Ginkaku-ji Temple
9   Nishiki-koji Food Market
10 Byodo-in Temple
11 Nara's Horyu-ji Temple

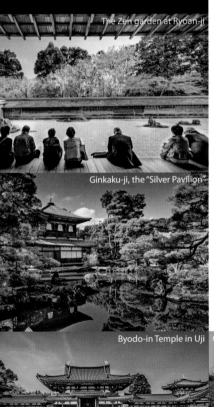

The Zen garden at Ryoan-ji

Ginkaku-ji, the "Silver Pavilion"

Byodo-in Temple in Uji

Geishas in the Gion district

MAKING THE MOST OF YOUR STAY

Part of the enduring charm of Kyoto and Nara is that no matter how long you stay or how often you return, Japan's former capitals always manage to keep providing something new to discover. One day it could be a temple garden you've previously missed, the next a new taste of Japan's culinary heritage or a snaking side street that leads into the past. Of course, most people don't have the luxury of spending a month or even a fortnight immersing themselves in the two cities, so what to do and see if (like most visitors) your time in Kyoto and Nara is short?

Your first day could start with two of Kyoto's star attractions, beginning with **Ryoan-ji** temple's cryptic Zen garden (page 10 for details of Ryoan-ji; Chapter 2, page 22 for the full day trip around Northwestern Kyoto) and then taking in the magnificent gilded temple of **Kinkaku-ji** (page 9) before heading to the gardens at the **Daitoku-ji** temple complex and finishing among the local crafts of the **Nishijin Textile Center** (page 24).

On your second day, you could wander from **Kiyomizu Temple** (page 11) through some of Kyoto's most atmospheric (and shop-filled) backstreets to **Chion-in Temple** (Chapter 2, page 26 for this day out). Another day could start at **Nijo Castle** (Chapter 2, page 33 for this day out), stop by **Kyoto Imperial Palace** (page 33) and then go shopping mad with a look around **Nishiki-koji food market** (page 34) to take in the city's culinary sights and smells and then more retail therapy in the **Teramachi arcade**, along **Shijo-dori** and in the **Kawaramachi** area.

Alternatively, you could opt for a visit to Kinkaku-ji's understated cousin, the sublime **Ginkaku-ji** (page 16) in northeastern Kyoto and then stroll the historic **Philosopher's Path** south toward the imposing **Heian Jingu** (with a possible detour to the **Nanzen-ji Temple** complex on route) before ending the day at the museums and galleries around **Okazaki-koen** (page 36 for this day out).

If you have time, you could also have a day trip south of Kyoto (Chapter 2, page 44) to visit the gardens of **Tofuku-ji Temple,** the sprawling **Fushimi Inari Shrine** and the town of **Uji**, known for its green tea and the site of the historic **Byodo-in Temple** (the temple on the back of the ¥10 coin). Or you could head west to the **Arashiyama** area (Chapter 2, page 40), which is most famous for its bamboo groves but also has some spectacular temples and shrines.

Then there is **Nara** (Chapter 2, page 48), Japan's capital before Kyoto in the 8th century and home to several World Heritage-designated temples. Whether you opt to visit as a day trip from Kyoto, as most people do, or take your time with an overnight stay, the city that is often called the "birthplace of Japanese civilization" adds a calming contrast to Kyoto. And for anyone who needs a break from tradition, Japan's second city, **Osaka** (page 52), can also be visited in a whirlwind day trip from Kyoto. Whichever options you choose, Kyoto and Nara won't disappoint.

1 Kinkaku-ji, the Golden Pavilion

The defining image of Kyoto, now a World Heritage Site

Whether it's accented by a light coating of snow in winter or basking in the clear blue skies of summer, the gilded temple of Kinkaku-ji remains a captivating sight year round. Nothing, save perhaps the sight of a *geisha* shuffling between teahouses in Gion, says "Kyoto" quite like it.

Originally built in 1397 as a villa for shogun Ashikaga Yoshimitsu, before being repurposed as a Zen temple after Yoshimitsu's death, what might come as a surprise is that the current incarnation of Kinkaku-ji only actually dates to the mid-1950s, the original having been burned down by a young monk in 1950—an event which sent Japan almost into national mourning. Once the shock waves had passed, however, it didn't take long for the temple to rise again. By 1955 it had been rebuilt to original specifications with the exception of the gilding that now covers the top two stories—that had to wait until 1987, when Japan's post-war economic miracle was in full swing.

While that gilding and the shimmering reflection it casts over the pond in front of Kinkaku-ji are undoubtedly the most striking features (and the main reason Kinkaku-ji is one of Kyoto's most-visited sights), the structure itself is also a fascinating blend of styles. The third story is in the traditional Chinese *cha'an* style, the second in the *buke-zukuri* (a style common with warrior aristocrat residences) and the first floor the 11th-century *shinden-zukuri* style. With all those components combining with such effect, it's not hard to see why, despite its age, Kinkaku-ji was one of the 17 sites in Kyoto that received joint World Heritage status in 1994.

Opening Times Daily from 9 a.m.–5 p.m. **Getting There** You can take bus #101 or #205 to the Kinkaku-ji Michi bus stop or #59 and #12 to the Kinkaku-ji Mae bus stop. It's a short, well-marked route to the temple from either bus stop. **Contact** www.shokoku-ji.jp **Admission Fee** ¥400. **While in the area** Combine a trip to Kinkaku-ji with a day out in northwestern Kyoto (page 22) that also takes in the Zen rock garden at Ryoan-ji, the gardens of Daitoku-ji, and the Nishijin Textile Center.

2 Ryoan-ji's Zen Rock Garden
Japan's most enigmatic sight

Before the tour buses begin their daily procession to Ryoan-ji, the fleeting calm before the storm at the temple offers early birds a moment of Zen contemplation in the peace and quiet the designer of Ryoan-ji's garden likely intended. And there's plenty to contemplate from the wooden steps beside the garden at this UNESCO World Heritage site. Despite years of study and argument, nobody knows for sure when the garden was made or who made it, nor can anybody agree on what the designer was trying to express.

The *karesansui* (dry landscape) garden only measures 30 by 10 meters (100 x 30 feet), but the cryptic manner in which its 15 rocks are arranged on a bed of off-white sand within that rectangle have been argued to represent all sorts of things—from small islands on an ocean to a tiger carrying a cub across a river and even a map of Chinese Zen monasteries. As for the who and when of the garden's creation, the garden was most likely created just after the bloody Onin War of 1467–77, after which much of Kyoto had to be rebuilt, and judging by the style and historical records the man behind it is most likely an artist and landscape gar-

dener called Soami, even though the names of other landscapers are carved into some of the garden's rocks.

Whoever it may have been, they have left a challenge for visitors. See if you can find a point from where you can see all 15 rocks at the same time. The designer has managed to lay out the rocks in such a way that you won't be able to see more than 14 at once, unless, it is said, you have reached the point of spiritual enlightenment. Most likely the only way to see all 15 is to check out the small replica of the garden on display just inside the main temple building; it won't bring enlightenment but it'll give you a better understanding of the sweeping patterns in the sand and the way the rocks have been grouped.

Opening Times Mar.–Nov. 8 a.m.–5 p.m., Dec.–Feb. 8.30 a.m.–4.30 p.m. **Getting There** Take buses #50 or #55 to the Ritsumeikan Daigaku-mae bus stop or bus #59 to Ryoanji-mae. Ryoan-ji is also a seven-minute walk from Ryoanji-michi Station on the Keifuku Kitano Line. **Contact** www.ryoanji.jp **Admission Fee** ¥500. **While in the area** After Ryoan-ji head to another of Kyoto's main attractions, the gilded Kinkaku-ji (pages 9 and 22), which is just over a kilometer to the northeast and easily reached by bus from Ryoan-ji.

3 Kiyomizu Temple
Tradition and nature—a view of Kyoto from on high

From *haiku* poetry to the (Chinese originated) concept of "borrowed scenery" in garden and architectural design, traditional Japanese culture is deeply rooted in an appreciation and reflection of nature and especially the seasons. Kiyomizu Temple in eastern Kyoto is a particularly fine example of that.

The temple's main hall (Hondo) has a backdrop that marks the seasons. In spring (the natural, academic and fiscal beginning to the year in Japan) the Hondo is accented by the delicate pinks of cherry blossom. Come summer, it's immersed in a sea of lush green that gives way to rich reds and yellows in autumn, before the foliage thins and is occasionally dappled with snow in winter.

Kiyomizu Temple is comprised of many elements (including a three-storied pagoda that is especially magical when occasionally illuminated at night), but it's the Hondo that steals the show. Dating to the 1600s, like many of Kiyomizu's current buildings (although the temple was established much earlier in 778), the hall is built on a rock face that overlooks a small valley and features a protruding wooden veranda held up by 12-meter

(40-foot) high *keyaki* (Japanese Zelkova) pillars.

Not only are the hall and its veranda one of Kyoto's most memorable images, a Japanese idiom equivalent to "take the plunge" was born from it. It used to be said that anyone who leapt from the overhanging veranda and survived would have their dreams answered, while anyone who died trying would be rewarded by sainthood. It might sound like everyone is a winner with that deal, but don't be tempted to leap yourself. Taking the plunge from Kiyomizu Temple was illegalized back in 1872 in response to a spate of leaping mishaps.

Opening Times The main hall is open daily from 6 a.m.–6 p.m. **Getting There** From Kyoto Station head to the Gojo-zaka bus stop, served by City Bus #100 and #206. Kiyomizu Temple is a ten-minute walk uphill from there (just follow the crowds). From the Kawaramachi and Shijo areas, you can catch City Bus #207 to the Kiyomizu-michi bus stop. **Contact** www.kiyomizudera.or.jp. **Admission Fee** ¥300. **While in the area** After the temple, check out the stores and cafes on the sloping Ninenzaka, Sannen-zaka, and Kiyomizuzaka streets nearby (page 26). You'll find lots of old craft shops and places to try traditional sweets.

4 Nijo Castle
An Edo-era symbol of the Shogun's power and prestige

Constructed in 1603 by the first Edo-era shogun, Tokugawa Ieyasu, Nijo Castle (Nijo-jo in Japanese) was born as a powerful statement of intent, serving as a potent reminder to all in Kyoto of Tokugawa strength. Although Ieyasu ruled from afar in Tokyo (then called Edo), the mighty Nijo-jo left no one in doubt that Big Brother was watching and ready to pounce.

Located in the heart of Kyoto, just northwest of Nishiki and Shijo (see page 33 for a full day out in the area), Nijo-jo's grounds are spread out over 275,000 m² (329,000 yd²) in which modern-day visitors will find a pair of palaces (the Hinomaru and the Ninomaru), remains of fortifications and landscaped gardens that together saw Nijo-jo granted World Heritage designation. In particular, it's the Ninomaru palace that stands out. Its gardens, designed by famed Edo-era landscape designer Kobori Enshu, combine pines (to symbolize longevity) and rocks (representing loyalty) to appease Tokugawa's ego, while inside the palace itself are some of the most ornate screen paintings and carvings in the country—the outer chambers, which would have been used for lower-ranked visitors, decorated with fear-inducing paintings that evoke strength and power, yet the inner chambers for trusted and higher-ranked guests being home to more calming, beautiful imagery.

Through the 265 years of Tokugawa rule, Nijo-jo's defenses were never put to the test, but should anyone have been brave enough to launch an attack, the remaining giant stone walls encircling the castle's grounds suggest that Nijo-jo would have withstood almost any onslaught. As for attacks more subtle, the artistry at the Ninomaru wasn't restricted to paintings on the walls and doors—ninja beware, as the "nightingale" floors in the Ninomaru palace are designed to squeak like birds should an intruder try to enter by stealth.

Opening Times Daily 8.45 a.m.–5 p.m. (last entry 4 p.m.). **Getting There** From Kyoto Station you can get City Bus #9, #50 or #101 to Nijo-jo-mae bus stop. The same bus stop can also be reached from Karasuma Station by City Bus #12 or #101. **Contact** www.city.kyoto.jp/bunshi/nijojo/english **Admission Fee** ¥600. **While in the area** Combine Niji-jo with the other sites featured in the tour of central Kyoto on page 33, including Kyoto Imperial Palace Park, Nishiki-koji food market, and the stores along Shijo-dori and in the Kawaramachi area.

5 Fushimi Inari Shrine
Kyoto at its mesmerizing best

Eye catching, enchanting, iconic—there are many ways to describe Fushimi Inari Taisha (shrine) in southern Kyoto. You could add "good exercise" to the list, too, if you decide to walk around the whole shrine.

Dating to the early 700s, Fushimi Inari Shrine is best known for its 10,000 vermilion *torii* gateways, which cover four kilometers (two and a half miles) of winding pathways that lead up and around a wooded mountain punctuated by small shrines and small fox statues, all combining to create an atmosphere that is at turns mystical, at others eerie, but always begging to be explored.

The grand scale of Fushimi Inari Shrine reflects its importance. It's the head shrine of some 40,000 other Inari shrines across Japan, all dedicated to one of Shinto's principal deities, Inari Okami, the god of rice, *sake*, prosperity, industry, fertility and numerous other things. Inari has certainly collected an impressive portfolio over the centuries. He or she has also collected numerous guises—Inari has been depicted as male and female, old and young, as a bodhisattva, and even

as a fox. It's the latter that often causes some confusion as the stone foxes scattered about Fushimi Inari Shrine are frequently called Inari, when in this case they are actually supposed to be just foxes (*kitsune*) acting as Inari's messengers.

If you were to come in early January, the shrine would be packed with people doing the traditional *hatsu-mode*—the first visit of the year to a shrine to offer prayers for good fortune for the year ahead. In fact, on any visit here, you will see a fairly steady flow of business people and others hoping for a little fortune from Inari. Whenever you visit, there's a good chance you won't find anywhere else in Kyoto to be quite as mesmerizing.

Opening Times Daily from dawn to dusk. **Getting There** About a 5-minute walk from Inari Station on the JR Nara Line or 10 minutes from Fushimi-Inari Station on the Keihan Line. For a day out in southern Kyoto that includes Fushimi Inari Shrine and other sights, see Chapter 2, page 44. **Contact** http://inari.jp **Admission Fee** Free. **While in the area** Do Fushimi Inari Shrine as a day out in southern Kyoto that also includes the gardens of Tofuku-ji Temple and the green tea and Byodo-in Temple in Uji (page 46).

6 The Gion District
Kyoto's famed geisha and entertainment district

Gion isn't the only place in Kyoto where you will find *geisha*, but it is the most famous. The backstreets here, lined with wooden *machiya* townhouses that serve as high-end restaurants and exclusive teahouses—lowly-lit lanterns hanging out front of an evening—provide the perfect backdrop for the white-faced *geisha* and their ornately decorated *kimono* as they flit between appointments.

Some of the *geisha* you see in Gion will be apprentices known as *maiko*, while some will be full *geisha* (referred to in Kyoto as *geiko*), who would have been through at least five years of training, not just in how to dress and behave like a *geisha*, but in traditional pastimes such as flower arranging, the tea ceremony, and performing arts. The question is: can you tell the difference? One way is to look at the belt. A *maiko*'s *kimono* belt (called an *obi*) will drop down at the back to almost touch the floor, while a *geiko* will have her *obi* neatly folded like a square on her back. The *maiko* might also have accessories in her hair, where a *geisha*

won't, and while a *geisha* will always wear flat *zori* sandals, you might also see a *maiko* in platformed footwear.

If you want to spot some *geiko* or *maiko*, be in Gion around 5.30pm to 6pm, when many are on their way to their evening appointments. Then follow some simple rules if you are going to try photographing them—don't block their path to get your shot (from behind or the side is ok), don't try and pose with them, don't stalk (some busloads of visitors do!) and don't photograph them if they are walking with a client.

Getting There From Kyoto Station, buses #100 and #206 run to the Gion bus stop. The area can also be accessed by Gion Shijo Station on the Keihan Line and (a slightly longer walk) Kawaramachi Station on the Hankyu Line. To explore Gion as part of a half-day out, see Chapter 2, page 30. **While in the area** You'd need some heavy connections and deep pockets to get into many of Gion's restaurants and teahouses, but not everything is pricey or off limits. Try Gion Tokuya (gion-tokyuya.jp) for green tea and sweets in traditional surrounds. Or, look at the *geisha* shows on page 66, if you are happy to drop a couple of hundred dollars on what will be an unforgettable night out.

7 Arashiyama's Bamboo Grove
A glimpse of Kyoto's sublime natural beauty

As Kyoto's attractions go, the bamboo grove in Arashiyama has to be one of the most beguilling. It's certainly one of the most photographed. Running between two of the Arashiyama area's other main attractions, Tenryu-ji and the Okochi-sanso Villa, strolling through the narrow walkways of the bamboo grove is simply enchanting. The light, often filtered a soft green through the towering bamboo's canopy, produces an otherworldly feel that seems to send visitors into a photographic trance. You can almost guarantee you will see someone lying on their back, camera to the sky, trying (usually in vain) to get a prime, people-free angle of the bamboo stalks as they gently sway in the breeze.

Then there's the sound. The eerie creaking noises the bamboo makes adds to the surreal sense of the place, so much so that the Ministry of the Environment has included the bamboo forest on its oddly-named "100 Soundscapes of Japan" list (one of countless, sometimes seemingly pointless

"100…of Japan" lists that the Japanese government and other organizations are quite fond of issuing). You just have to make sure you don't get stuck between high-school touring groups or you won't hear anything but chatter.

One thing to note before visiting is that the bamboo forest won't take much more than 30 minutes (maybe much less), so don't plan on heading out to Arashiyama just for it. Do it as part of a longer walk around Arashiyama (see page 40 for that). Like many other popular sights in Kyoto, try to get there early, too, as that will give you the best chance of not sharing the bamboo with busloads of tour groups.

Opening Times Dawn to dusk daily. **Getting There** About a ten-minute walk from Saga Arashiyama Station on the JR Sagano Line or Keifuku Arashiyama Station on the Randen Line. **Admission Fee** Free. **While in the area** Follow the half-day tour on page 40 to explore more of Arashiyama, which includes Tenryu-ji and the plush Okochi-sanso Villa, and also some nice stores and a footbath to finish at the station.

8 Ginkaku-ji Temple
The Silver(less) Pavilion

Kinkaku-ji's unadorned cousin, Ginkaku-ji, has got the natural look down pat. The Silver Pavilion, as it's often known in English (*Gin* means silver), was supposedly going to be covered in silver leaf when it was built as a shogun's retirement villa during the 1480s, but for reasons nobody can decide on today that never happened.

It's most likely that shogun Ashikaga Yoshimasa, the man behind Ginkaku-ji's construction (and the grandson of Ashikaga Yoshimitsu, who was responsible for the gilded Kinkaku-ji), simply ran out of money to fund the project, while others speculate that he never had any real intention of spending a fortune on all that silver. Whatever the reason, Ginkaku-ji, which became a Zen temple (officially called Jisho-ji) after Yoshimasa's death, is fine just the way it is.

Yoshimasa was said to have been a great patron of the arts, promoting such pursuits as poetry and the tea ceremony, which he pursued in his retirement at Ginkaku-ji, and the temple's understated beauty is certainly more representative of Japanese artistic sensibilities than the brashness of Kinkaku-ji. The view over Ginkaku-ji from the small wooded hill within the temple's grounds is worthy of a *haiku*. The grounds are lush with moss and trees that contrast with the simple raked sand garden, where the raised ripples in the white sand are said to be designed to reflect the moon's rays. The pond positioned in front of Ginkaku-ji sometimes ripples in the breeze, too, as its catches reflections of the two-story thatched temple. It all combines to make Ginkaku-ji uniquely special.

Opening Times Daily Mar.–Nov. 8.30 a.m.–5 p.m., Dec.–Feb. 9 a.m.–4.30 p.m. **Getting There** Take buses #5, #17 or #100 to the Ginkakuji-mae bus stop. Or look at Chapter 2, page 36, to see how Ginkaku-ji can be combined with a stroll along the nearby Philosopher's Path. **Contact** www.shokoku-ji.jp **Admission Fee** ¥500. **While in the area** After Ginkaku-ji walk down the Philosopher's Path as part of the day out detailed on page 36. The Philosopher's Path has a few nice cafes and stores on and just off it including Yojiya, where you can sip tea on *tatami* accompanied by some lovely garden views (page 37).

9 Nishiki-koji Food Market
Kyoto's oldest market is a sensory delight

To stroll along the approximately 500-meter (1,640-foot) covered street that makes up Nishiki-koji food market is to journey through the colors, aromas and flavors of Kyoto's culinary heritage. Running parallel to Shijo Street, one block to the north, the vibrant Nishiki-koji began life in 1616 as a fish market, but over the centuries its scope has broadened to encapsulate an incredible range of regional specialties and traditional traders.

For visitors with a sweet tooth, you'll find Swiss *baumkauchen* cake with a green tea flavored twist, colorful hard candies that look like ornate marbled glass, and traditional Japanese sweets such as *dango* (rice flour dumpling), *warabi mochi* (a thick, jelly-like sweet made with bracken starch) and *manju* (dough buns filled with red bean paste). In keeping with Nishiki's seafood roots, there are also stores that specialize in river fish, dried fish and cured fish, while among the rest of Nishiki's 126 stores you'll also find tofu and *yuba* (tofu skin) variations, pickles that come in almost

every conceivable color, a variety of handmade noodles, not to mention simple greengrocers, and several cafes and eateries. There's even cheap and cheerful *b-kyu gurume* (lit. b-grade gourmet) on hand in the shape of *tako-yaki* (octopus chunks deep-fried in batter), amongst other things.

When it's too wet or too hot outside for temple hopping, an hour or two in the market should be at the top of your list of things to do. Whatever the weather, Nishiki-koji delivers a treat for the senses and an insight into Kyoto's culinary traditions.

Opening Times Daily 10 a.m.–5 p.m., although some stores have fixed days off. **Getting There** A several-minute walk from Shijo Station (Karasuma subway line), Karasuma Station (Hankyu Line) and Kawaramachi Station (Hankyu Line). Also handily served by City Bus #5 via the Shijo Takakura bus stop. **Contact** www.kyoto-nishiki.or.jp **Admission Fee** Free. **While in the area** Connected to Nishiki is the covered Teramachi arcade (page 33), a great place to browse craft shops, art galleries, book shops and many other places that offer things above and beyond typical tourist fare.

10 Byodo-in Temple
The historic "Phoenix Hall" and its priceless treasures

If you have a ¥10 coin handy, flip it over and you'll see one of Japan's most recognizable historic buildings—Byodo-in's Phoenix Hall spreading its wings as if about to take flight. Located south of Kyoto, in the town of Uji (page 44 for a day trip), the Phoenix Hall makes it onto modern-day currency for good reason. Not only is the design so striking, it's the only structure at Byodo-in Temple that dates to the temple's original construction in 1052-1053, when Fujiwara no Yorimichi, the son of the then emperor's closest adviser, decided to convert an old aristocrat's villa into a Buddhist temple.

While the outside of the Phoenix Hall leaves many visitors in a photographic frenzy, snapping away at the hall and its watery reflection, the inside of the hall is just as impressive thanks to a collection of exquisite historic artwork. Most notably that includes a seated statue of the Amitabha Tathagata Buddha sculpted by Heian-era (794-1185) master sculptor of Buddhist images Jocho, which was enshrined inside the hall in 1053 to celebrate its construction.

As a reminder that despite the temple's beauty, brutality was never all that far away in classical Japan, look out for a fan-shaped marker on the temple's grounds placed to mark the spot where prominent aristocrat and poet Minamoto no Yorimasa committed ritual suicide in the 12th century after losing control of Byodo-in Temple in battle against the Taira clan. The Minamoto clan would go on to win the resulting Genpei War against the Taira and with it rule Japan under the Kamakura shogunate (1192-1333), although in his death poem Yorimasa must have feared all was lost: Like an old tree / From which we gather no blossoms / Sad has been my life / Fated to bear no fruit.

Opening Times Daily 8.30 a.m.–5.30 p.m. The Phoenix Hall viewing sessions (every 20 minutes; maximum of 50 people at a time) run from 9.10 a.m.–4.30 p.m.
Getting There A ten-minute walk from Uji Station, which is 16 minutes from Kyoto on the JR Nara Line.
Contact www.byodoin.or.jp **Admission Fee** ¥600, plus an additional ¥300 to go inside the Phoenix Hall.
While in the area Uji is famed for tea and the streets that lead to Byodo-in Temple are lined with small stores that sell all manner of green tea inspired goods. On a hot day, try one of the slightly bitter green tea ice creams, or pick up an unusual souvenir like green tea liqueur or green tea noodles.

11 Nara's Horyu-ji Temple
An early outpost of Japanese Buddhism

Deciding on just one 'Don't Miss' to represent Nara is the kind of task that can leave a man awake at night. You could pick Todai-ji Temple (page 50), which is famous in part for its 15-meter (50-foot)-high bronze statue of Buddha, or maybe you could opt for Kofuki-ji Temple (page 48) because of its 600-year-old five-story pagoda, the original of which was moved to Nara from Kyoto in the 8th century. Then there is Horyu-ji Temple, which is home to not only an even older five-story pagoda, but also a building called the Kon-do (Golden Hall) that's believed to have been built around 670 AD, thereby making it the world's oldest wooden building. It almost came down to a game of Japan's favorite decision maker, *janken* (rock, paper, scissors), but in the end, age won out.

Founded in 607 AD, 50 years after Buddhism first arrived in Japan, Horyu-ji Temple was a major base from which the recently imported religion Buddhism spread across Japan under the patronage of Horyu-ji's founder Prince Shotoku (574–622 AD). While the complex and its ancient structures are an obvious main attraction (with a scale and splendor that

serve to highlight how quickly and deeply Buddhism established itself in Japan), Horyu-ji Temple is also known for its treasures. Some of Japanese Buddhism's most precious relics are kept at Horyu-ji's Kon-do today, including the original Medicine Buddha that Shotoku supposedly built Horyu-ji Temple to hold and a bronze image of Buddha dated to 623, while in the 8th-century Yumedono building in the complex's eastern precinct is the jewel in Horyu-ji's crown: a 178.8-cm (5-foot 10-inch-high) statue thought to be a life-size replica of Prince Shotoku, and which for centuries was kept hidden from all under a white cloth, only finally being uncovered in 1884.

Opening Times Daily 8 a.m.–4.30 p.m. **Getting There** Nara is 40 minutes from Kyoto on the Kintetsu-Kyoto Line's Limited Express and can also be reached by JR Lines from Kyoto and Osaka. The JR Yamatoji Line runs from JR Nara Station to Horyu-ji Temple (12 mins). **Contact** www.horyuji.or.jp **Admission Fee** ¥1,500. **While in the area** Look at the full guide to Nara (page 48), which will also take you to places like Todai-ji Temple (mentioned above) as well as the historic Nara-machi area (page 50) and its old wooden buildings that now house a great selection of craft stores, cafes and restaurants.

Ginkaku-ji Temple

Arashiyama

Ryoan-ji Temple

Byodo-in Temple

CHAPTER 2
EXPLORING KYOTO & NARA

Nishiki-koji food market

Kiyomizu Temple

You could explore Japan's two ancient capitals for years and still keep discovering new facets of the cities' rich past and present with each visit. To encounter the most memorable and worthwhile of places and experiences in both, we've broken Kyoto, Nara and nearby areas into nine different (mostly) day-long excursions, starting with a day that takes in Ryoan-ji and Kinkaku-ji temples and finally a day trip or overnighter to Nara. In case you need a break from tradition, we've also included a whirlwind day trip to Japan's second city, the always energetic Osaka.

Ryoan-ji Temple's Zen rock garden

NORTHWESTERN KYOTO
World Heritage temples Ryoan-ji and Kinkaku-ji and traditional crafts

See pull-out map H7; P15

When **Ryoan-ji** temple in northwestern Kyoto opens its doors at 8 a.m., there's a brief window of opportunity to have one of Kyoto's most photographed sights almost to yourself. Before the bus tours descend, bringing groups of school children and tour parties following their flag-carrying guides, you can imagine what it would have been like centuries ago to sit on the wooden decking outside the temple's small, main building and contemplate the meaning behind Ryoan-ji's famed Zen rock garden. Theories abound about the placement of the rocks and the way the garden is raked (see page 10), but what is undisputed is how captivating the small (it's only 30 by 10

meters/100 x 30 feet) patch of landscaping can be. If you get to Ryoan-ji early enough, just ten minutes of peace and quiet here is a great way to start a day exploring the main sights of north and northwest Kyoto.

You won't need more than 30 to 45 minutes to check out the garden at Ryoan-ji and then stroll around its pond, so afterwards head on to **Kinkaku-ji** (page 9) and you might also miss the worst of the crowds there. To get there you can walk north-east for 20 minutes through fairly nondescript areas, hop into one of the taxis loitering outside of Ryoan-ji or catch buses #12 or #59 to Kinkaku-ji Michi bus stop. Even if you get there later in the day and end up sharing the gilded Kinkaku-ji with hundreds of others, it is still more than worth a visit. Built in the Muromachi Period (1337-1573—a halcyon age for garden design in Japan—this Zen temple is another attraction that, once there, doesn't really need much more than 30 to 45 minutes, because the main event is simply to stand and stare at the magnificent gilded pavilion as it casts its shimmering reflection into the landscaped pond that stretches out before it. All year it is a stunning sight, whether dusted with snow or backed by lush summer greenery under blue skies.

Far less crowded is the **Daitoku-ji temple complex** (open dawn to dusk; free, but individual gardens charge a fee), which makes a good next stop on a day out in northwest Kyoto. Comprised of more than 20 temples, slowly strolling around Daitoku-ji offers a window into the calm world of Zen and in particular Zen landscaping and layout. The eponymous Daitoku-ji itself, which was founded in the 1300s (though the oldest buildings date to the 1500s) is a study of classic Zen planning, with a giant two-tier gateway (the Sanmon), a Buddha Hall (Butsuden), a sutra library (Kyozo), Abbot's quarters (Hojo), and Dharma hall (Hatto). The gardens in some of the subtemples, however, are the highlight of Daitoku-ji. Set in a bamboo grove, the mossy garden at **Koto-in** temple (¥400;

Kinkaku-ji

at 9 a.m.–4.30 p.m.) is especially pretty when accented by autumn colors and it has a lovely *tatami* mat area that opens up to a wooden veranda from which to take it all in. Likewise the *karesansui* (dry landscaped garden) at **Daisen-in**

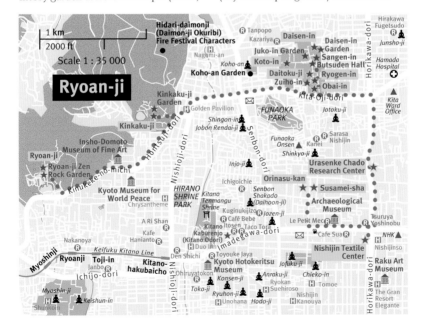

Ryogen-in Temple

(¥400; at least 9 a.m.–4.30 p.m) capti-vates with a cryptic raked layout like that at Ryoan-ji, while other sub-temples like **Ryogen-in** (¥350; 9 a.m.–4.30 p.m.) and **Obai-in** (open only in spring and fall; ¥600) manage to combine bamboo grove, ancient mossy paths and dry landscaping to striking effect. Time and admission

The entrance to Koto-in

fees make visiting all of them a no-no for most people, so if there is time for just one, I'd opt for Koto-in or Obai-in.

After Ryoan-ji, Kinkaku-ji and Daitoku-ji (if you do them all), you could be for-given for being "templed out". Nearby **Nishijin**, Kyoto's historic textile center, is a nice change of scene. About one kilo-meter south of Daitoku-ji, a good place to start exploring Nishijin is at the **Nishijin Textile Center** (www.nishijin.or.jp), which as well as having fabrics on dis-play and hosting weaving demonstra-tions, has almost hourly *kimono* shows and (at a cost) the opportunity to have a go at weaving and try on *kimono*. Yes, it is touristy, but it is still a fun introduc-tion to Nishijin's 1,000-year fabric his-tory, and they also have quite a lot of *kimono* and other fabrics on sale. Away from the textile center the Nishijin dis-trict itself is a pleasant place to walk around, with the area's old *machiya* houses often providing an atmospheric old location to stop for something to eat or

Matcha green tea served with a sweet

tea ceremony and such things as tea ceremony utensils.

Just be noted that it's not the kind of place you can pop into for a one-off tea ceremony experience in English; for that, have a look at page 78 (Best Cultural Experiences) in Chapter 3, where we've listed a few of the best teahouses that offer easily accessible tea ceremony classes and experiences.

drink—places like the former bathhouse turned cafe **Sarasa Nishijin** (sarasan2. exblog.jp; noon–11 p.m.; closed Wed; about 500m/1,640 ft south of Daitokuji).

There are also places to get a less touristy look at Nishijin's textiles. **Orinasu-kan** (Tues to Sun, 10 a.m.–4 p.m.; ¥500) is a lovely little museum focused on Nishijin textiles that is housed in an old textile workshop, and across the road there is a small gallery (**Susamei-sha**) that exhibits a beautiful collection of *kimono*. Also in the area is the **Urasenke Chado Research Center** (www.urasenke. or.jp), the nation's largest tea ceremony school, which has good exhibitions on the

Main sights The Zen garden at Ryoan-ji, the gilded Kinkaku-ji, the gardens at the Daitoku-ji temple complex, and the Nishijin Textile Center. **Time Required** At least half a day and it is best to start early to avoid the crowds. **Getting There** Start at Ryoan-ji, which is served by bus #59 (Ryoan-ji mae bus stop) and #55 or #50 (both Ritsumeikan Daigaku-mae bus stop; 7-minute walk). **Where to Eat** Wait until you are in the Daitoku-ji and Nishijin areas, as there are quite a few nice cafes and restaurants there that are housed in traditional buildings. **Insider Tip** For a bit of variety, this part of Kyoto is also home to the kitschy Eigamura (page 75), the theme park run by the TOEI movie studios. Some 200 films and TV shows are shot each year in the Edo era–themed sets here, so you might see some movie action while strolling around (in Edo-era costumes if the urge takes you). Whether there is filming going on or not, the daily ninja shows are very over-the-top and well worth watching.

Kimono fashion at the Nishijin Textile Center

SOUTHEASTERN KYOTO
Exploring Kyoto's atmospheric backstreets from Kiyomizu to Chion-in

See pull-out map L10–L9; Q16

The southern Higashiyama area of Kyoto, located east of central Kyoto over the Kamogawa River and with wooded hills lining its eastern side, is packed with attractions all within easy walking distance of each other, from the World Heritage-designated Kiyomizu Temple and the lanes full of old stores that lead off it, to the historic Yasaka Shrine, Maruyama Park and Chion-in Temple.

A good place to start a walk around the area is **Kiyomizu Temple** (see Getting There at the end of this section for directions and page 11, for a fuller write-up),

which was established at the foot of the Higashiyama mountains at the end of the eighth century, but like many other Kyoto sites now mostly dates to the 1600s. The stand-out attraction here is one of those 17th-century buildings, the Hondo (main hall), which is defined in part by a protruding 12-meter (40-foot) high wooden veranda that overlooks a small valley and in part by a seasonally changing backdrop that during spring is colored with cherry blossoms, in winter might take on a thin white coat of snow, and (best of all) in fall is engulfed by rich earthy tones.

Leading downhill from Kiyomizu Temple is Kiyomizu-zaka, which soon connects (turning right and heading north) to the Sannen-zaka and Ninen-zaka lanes, both of which are lined with wooden buildings that house traditional shops, teahouses, and other places to stop for refreshments. This is how more of Kyoto should be—a carefully preserved pedestrian-only route that feels as if it winds back in time—and it's worth taking

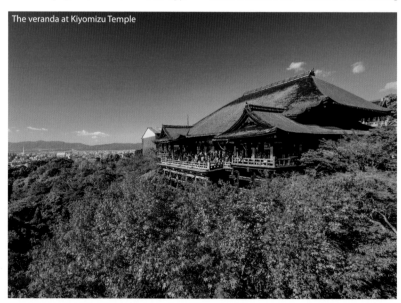
The veranda at Kiyomizu Temple

your time here to take it all in. Go slowly and you'll find shops like Asahido (page 71) close to Kiyomizu Temple, which specialize in Kyoto ceramics, as well as places like the teahouse Kasagiya (no website) near the northern end of Ninen-zaka, where for around ¥1,000 you can take green tea and traditional sweets in a charming old townhouse. If you get hungry around here for something more filling, there's also a branch of the noodle restaurant **Omen** (the main branch is covered on page 64, near Ginkaku-ji) right at the northern end of Ninen-zaka.

Keep heading north and it's only half a kilometer or so to **Yasaka Shrine** (www. yasaka-jinja.or.jp; free) and the neighboring **Maruyama Park**. As the host of the

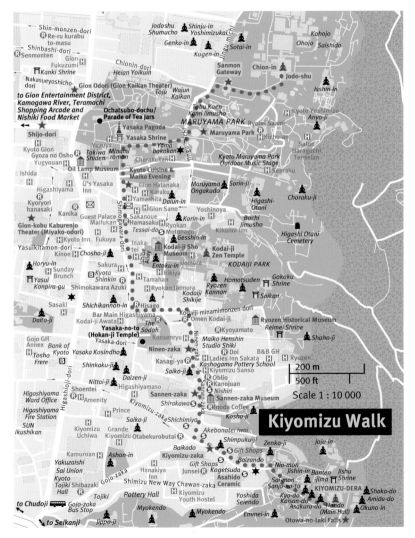

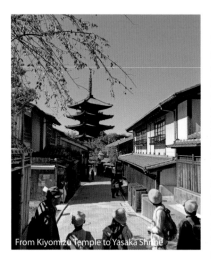

From Kiyomizu Temple to Yasaka Shrine

First built in the late 7th century (but now with much more modern reconstructions), Yasaka marks the end of Shijo-dori (see page 33) with its striking orange and white two-tiered gateway, through which a steady stream of visitors pass to reach the shrine's simple main hall and lantern-adorned dance stage, the light of which gives the shrine's grounds a calming glow at night. Although the characters written on the several hundred lanterns here can look quite exotic and mystical, like shrine lanterns the country over, these simply bear the names of people and businesses who have donated money to the shrine—not that they look any the less for that.

historic Gion Matsuri in July (see Festivals & Events, page 77), when a procession of floats accompanied by traditional music set off from Yasaka, the shrine is especially vibrant with array of side events and food stalls attracting hundreds of thousands of visitors while the festival runs its course. Year round, however, the shrine is still well worth a visit.

Adjoining the shrine is Maruyama Park, a nice place most of the year to have a break from sightseeing, but an especially good one in late March and early spring to join locals for a spot of cherry blossom viewing. As the *sakura* blooms in various shades of pink, *hanami* (blossom-viewing) parties take place under the petals across Japan, picnic sheets spread out, *bento*

Cherry blossom season in Maruyama Park

The Sanmon gateway at Chion-in Temple

lunch boxes, beer and *sake* on hand to fuel the festivities. Maruyama Park ranks as one of the prettiest and liveliest places for the annual event in Kyoto.

Leaving the park behind, you have two good choices. You could follow the rest of this section and head northward to Chion-in Temple (which is also near Tea Ceremony En, page 78, if you get the urge to try a tea ceremony in English). Or, you could flip to page 30 for the Exploring Gion section and head west into Kyoto's old dining, entertainment and *geisha* hub. Let's look here at Chion-in Temple (www.chion-in.or.jp/e; 9 a.m.–4p.m.; free, but 500 yen to enter the temple's two gardens), a temple complex located just to the north of Maruyama Park.

Built in the 1200s, but with most of its structures now dating to the 1600s, traditional temple life at Chion-in Temple seems to go on undisturbed by the thousands of visitors that pass through each day; in particular the thick smell of incense and sound of chanting monks gives the main hall of this sprawling complex an otherworldly feel, while the scale of some of the structures speaks volumes to Chion-in's importance as the

head temple of Jodo-shu Buddhism (Pure Land Buddhism), which was founded by the monk Honen in 1175. The main hall (Mieido) is an impressive, squat 45-meter (150-foot) long structure that houses a golden altar, but so too are the 24-meter (80-foot) tall, 50-meter (165-foot) wide Sanmon gateway, which the pamphlet to the temple describes perfectly with the phrase "solemn magnificence", and the temple's 400-year-old, 3-meter (10-foot) high bell.

Main sights The World Heritage-designated Kiyomizu Temple, the atmospheric and store-lined Kiyomizu-zaka, Ninen-zaka and Sannen-zaka streets, Yasaka Shrine, Maruyama Park, and Chion-in Temple. **Time Required** Half a day or longer. **Getting There** From Kyoto Station head to the Gojo-zaka bus stop, served by City Bus #100 and #206. Kiyomizu Temple is a ten-minute walk uphill from there. From the Kawaramachi and Shijo areas, you can also catch City Bus #207 to the Kiyomizu-michi bus stop. From both bus stops it's easy to find your way; just follow the crowds. **Insider Tip** This tour is done entirely on foot, so wear something comfortable on your feet and take precautions for heatstroke on a hot and humid day (summer in Kyoto can drain you quickly without you noticing).

Chion-in Temple

EXPLORING GION
Kyoto's traditional dining and entertainment hub

See pull-out map B3–C4

As darkness falls in the early Kyoto evening there is nowhere quite as magical as the old streets of the Gion area. Lanterns hang outside of wooden buildings that serve as teahouses and restaurants, ornately dressed *geisha* shuffle between appointments; even if you are there for just a few moments, it really is the quintessential Kyoto experience. In fact, by day or by night, Gion is easily worth several hours of aimless

wandering. My suggestion would be to come at around 5 p.m, (a good time for *geisha* and *maiko* spotting) after having spent the day taking in either the walk around Central Kyoto (page 33) or the

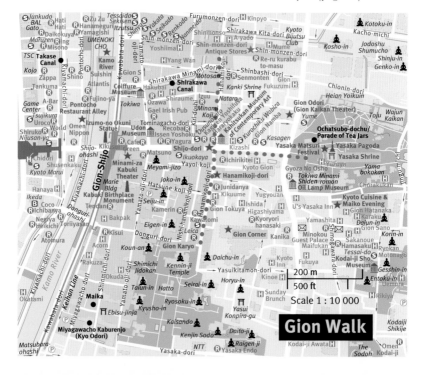

Gion Walk

200 m
500 ft
Scale 1 : 10 000

Gion sidestreets

walk around Southeastern Kyoto (page 26). Equally, however, you could do Gion with one of the guided walking tours mentioned on page 88 or stroll around by yourself at any time of the day or night. Just make sure you visit the area at some point during your time in Kyoto.

So, where to start? Head for Shijo-dori, where about 100 meters (330 feet) west of Yasaka Shrine (at the far eastern end of Shijo) you'll come to an intersection where Hanamikoji-dori, Gion's main street, cuts north-south across the road. If you were to follow this north (right), in about five minutes you would get to **Shinmonzen-dori** and Kyoto's best collection of antique shops (covered in detail on page 72), where the several dozen stores specialize in everything from Imari ceramic ware and Buddhist paintings to calligraphy items and scrolls to Edo-era furniture and swords. Even if you aren't interested in taking home an antique, it's worth giving yourself an hour here just to experience the craftsmanship and scope of traditional Japanese arts and crafts (note that many shops will close by 6 p.m. or 7 p.m.).

Head south down Hanamikoji-dori and you step back in time. The old wooden

buildings here, some with *noren* curtains flitting in front of their entrances, others with lanterns out front, are home to some of Kyoto's most exclusive *geisha* teahouses and restaurants—the kind of places where one needs a big budget and a personal introduction from a regular customer to get in—but thanks to tourism there are also places here to get a genuine taste of Gion on a normal budget. One hundred meters south from Shijo-dori (on your left) is **Gion Tokuya** (noon–6 p.m.; gion-tokuya.jp; average ¥1,500), where anyone can pop in for green tea and sweets in a traditional *tatami* mat room. Further on, in a lovely two-story wooden *machiya* house, camera maker Leica has a small store and gallery (free; 11 a.m.–7 p.m.) that gives a good chance to check out the inside of this kind of building and very often great photos of Kyoto. Next to it is a traditional restaurant called **Karyo**, which serves good *kaiseki* at lunch for an (relatively speaking) affordable ¥5,000 (11.30 a.m.–1 p.m.; dinners from ¥10,000; www.karyo-kyoto.jp/gion). Also accessible to all at this end of Hanamikoji-dori is **Gion Corner** (page 66), which puts on a fun revue that includes *geisha* dancing,

A geisha performance

traditional theater and other performing art—an unashamedly touristy experience, but still a really good way to see a variety of Japanese arts in one sitting and without breaking your budget. If you wanted something more authentic (and be prepared to pay a lot), Gion has high-end *geisha* shows, too; have a look at **Geisha Shows** on page 66 for a rundown of the options in and near Gion, from Gion Corner to a ¥100,000+ night out.

Of course, dinner in and around Gion doesn't have to include *geisha*. Actually, let's be honest, it rarely does except for special occasions. For me, if I am going to splurge on dinner, nothing—absolutely nothing—comes close to *kaiseki* in Kyoto. It's not just the food. It's the combination of seasonal flavors, artful presentation, traditional setting, attentive *kimono*-clad service, and so many other small factors that together form a remarkable culinary experience. At the best *kaiseki* restaurants, each course makes you feel special; from that "wow" moment as it arrives in front of you to the tentative first taste, when you feel almost guilty for destroying the art work, and then

through to the sometimes subtle, sometimes bold flavors that leave you at a loss for words. If you are going to do *kaiseki* in Kyoto, do it in Gion. It can sometimes be hard to snag a reservation (so try to book well in advance), but if you can, try **Minokou** (full review on page 61), **Kyoto-Gion Nanba** (kyotonanba.com) or **Gion Hatanaka** (where the *kaiseki* dinner is paired with a *geisha* show; page 66) and you won't regret the size of the bill. Don't forget also that many high-end restaurants, including the three just listed, have value sampler sets available at lunch, where for ¥3,500 to ¥5,000 you get a great introduction to *kaiseki* without having to invest in the full ¥20,000-something dinner experience.

Main sights The Gion district itself, *kaiseki* restaurants, antique stores, and *geisha* shows. **Time Required** Just a couple of hours. **Getting There** From Kyoto Station, buses #100 and #206 run to the Gion bus stop. The area can also be accessed by Gion Shijo Station on the Keihan Line and (a slightly longer walk) Kawaramachi Station on the Hankyu Line. **Insider Tip** Gion is great by day or night, but it's extra special of an evening. Try one of the days out in Central Kyoto (page 33) or Southeastern Kyoto (page 26) and then head on to Gion as night begins to fall.

CENTRAL KYOTO
Nijo Castle, Kyoto Imperial Palace and the Kawaramachi Shopping District

See pull-out map J8–L10

Early in the 1600s the first Edo-era shogun, Tokugawa Ieyasu, built **Nijo Castle** in central Kyoto to serve both as his official residence and as a symbol of the power of the new shogunate, which would go on to rule Japan for the next 260 years. While the original castle, which Ieyasu's grandson Iemitsu expanded with an imposing five-story keep, is no longer fully intact, the site is still home to gardens and fine palace buildings (complete with anti-ninja nightingale floors) that make it one of Kyoto's most popular sites—the perfect place to start a day-long tour of central Kyoto that includes **Kyoto Imperial Palace** and shopping areas like Nishiki-koji food market, the covered **Teramachi arcade** and the department stores in Kawaramachi.

Nijo Castle itself is covered in more detail on page 12. When you are done there, from the castle's southeast corner it's a 500-meter (1,640–foot) walk east (nine blocks in all) to the **Kyoto International Manga Museum**—an unmissable site for any comic or animation fan, or anyone interested in Japanese pop culture. Housed in an old school building, the museum has about 300,000 comics in its collection, mostly from Japan but also from other countries, which visitors can pick up and read. There are also occasional cartoon drawing demos and other events.

From the *manga* museum the next major sight in central Kyoto is **Kyoto Imperial Palace Park** another 500 meters (1,640 feet) away, straight up Karasuma-dori. The main tourist attraction here are the daily tours of the inner Palace grounds and garden (the only way to get inside is to apply for the tour, but it's free: sankan.kunaicho.go.jp/english/guide/kyoto), although many people find them a bit of a miss because of the sheer number of people on the hour-long guided tour and because the tour doesn't actually go inside any of the buildings; for others the insight provided by the guides brings the buildings, which date to the

Imperial Palace Park

mid-1850s but are a mix of architectural styles from other eras, to life. For me, the main reason to head to the palace area is to enjoy the parkland that surrounds the walled-off palace grounds. The lawns and tree groves in this huge rectangular slab of green (it's about 1,300 by 800 meters/1420 x 875 yards) are a lovey place to unwind—great for small kids to run about in too—and are home to a small shrine and pretty landscaped garden.

Then directly across the road from the southeast corner of the palace grounds comes the start of **Teramachi Street**, which runs all the way south down to Shijo-dori (about 750 meters/half a mile) and includes the covered Teramachi arcade, a shopping area that has its roots

in the 16th century. While many of the stores are the things you'd find in any neighborhood, many reveal the street's roots—beside clothing stores and other modern outlets like bookstores and even a *manga* store, many of the shops have been here for generations, specializing in such things as incense, prayer beads, antiques (see page 72 for more on antique shopping), and crafts. Near the arcade's southern end (a block before reaching Shijo-dori) Teramachi intersects with **Nishiki-koji food market** (page 17), which also traces its roots to the 16th century. Running parallel to the busiest part of Shijo-dori the 500-meter (1,640-foot) covered shopping street is home to a wonderful range of traditional

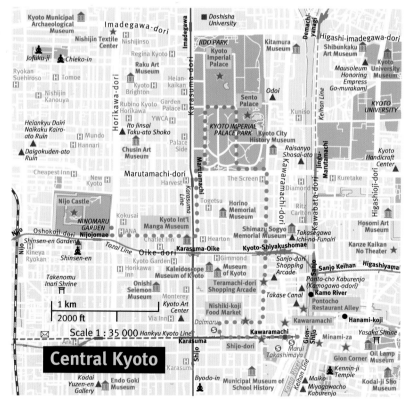

Central Kyoto

Kyoto flavors; from sweets to savory fish to pickles. Just beyond its western end there are also a couple of nice places for lunch; just on the right once the covered market ends **Otoya** (which has a picture menu) sells nicely balanced *teishoku* set meals for around ¥1,000 while another 50 meters (165 feet) on (and on the left) **Ippudo** is one of Kyoto's most well-known *ramen* joints.

Head a block south from here to Shijo-dori and the shops become more modern, with department stores like Daimaru (10 a.m.–8 p.m. daily), Marui (10.30 a.m.–8.30 p.m. daily) and Takashimaya (10 a.m.–8 p.m. daily) all located on the 500-meter (1,640-foot) main shopping stretch of Shijo-dori that runs between the Karasuma-Shijo intersection east to the **Kawaramachi intersection**. All three are giants, with multiple floors featuring brand-name fashions and accessories, restaurants and cafes, but also with great basement food courts that are worth a visit in their own right. Besides selling a great variety of *bento* lunch boxes, these *depaachika* floors also sell deli goods, patisseries, chocolates, traditional sweets, rice crackers, cakes, drinks, pickles, and many local specialties that make them a real treat for the senses.

After shopping, the Kawaramachi intersection is close to plenty of good evening options. You could cross the river and check out a traditional show at the **Minami-za** kabuki theater (page 67), or walk a few hundred meters further for the entrance to the old Gion district (covered on page 30), which is lovely to stroll at night and has plenty of places (like Minokou, page 61) to try *kaiseki* cuisine. Alternatively, you could try dinner in the old Pontocho area, a lovely narrow alley of restaurants, stores, watering holes and teahouses running between Shijo-dori

Restaurants facing the Kamogawa

and Sanjo-dori a block to the west of the river. Pedestrian only, **Pontocho-dori** and its old wooden buildings are especially pretty after dark, offering plenty of places to try traditional cuisine in atmospheric settings. To call out just a few, consider a night at **Toriume** (www.tori-ume.net; the ¥4,000 fixed course makes ordering easy) for affordable char-grilled chicken (*yakitori*) and a great range of *sake*, **Fujita** (www.pontocho-fujita.jp; courses from ¥7,200) for seasonal *kaiseki* sat low on *tatami*-mat ted flooring or at counter seats where you can watch the chefs at work, or (with money no issue) somewhere like **Misoguigawa** (www.misogui.jp/eng; ¥30,000 fixed course) for its fusion of French and *kaiseki* cuisines served up in a charming former teahouse.

Main sights Shijo-dori avenue and Kawaramachi, the covered Nishiki-koji food market and Teramachi shopping arcade, the Pontocho area, Kyoto International Manga Museum, Kyoto Imperial Palace Park, Nijo Castle. **Time Required** A full day. **Getting There** From Kyoto Station you can get City Bus #9, #50 or #101 to Nijo-jo-mae bus stop. The same bus stop can also be reached from Karasuma Station by City Bus #12 or #101. **Insider Tip** At the end of the day you could easily visit the Gion area, Kyoto's most famous *geisha* district, which is very close to Kawaramachi and covered on page 30.

Ginkaku-ji's dry landscaped garden

NORTHEASTERN KYOTO
A walk through Kyoto's past from Ginkaku-ji to Heian Jingu

See pull-out map L8–M9

Northeastern Kyoto doesn't have the same concentration of sights as the downtown area, but being home to one of the city's most beautiful temples and a pretty walking route that leads past many notable temples, the Heian Jingu shrine and a collection of interesting museums, the area makes one of the nicest half-day walks Kyoto has to offer.

It's a walk that starts at **Ginkaku-ji**, the understated cousin of the gilded Kinkaku-ji in Northwestern Kyoto (page 22). Sometimes called the Silver Pavilion, (*Gin* means silver; *kin* gold), the temple dates to the late 1400s when, like Kinkaku-ji, it was built as a shogun's retirement villa. Unlike Kinkaku-ji, which as its name suggests is covered in gold, however, Ginkaku-ji never got its silver-leaf coating, and the result is a lovely natural look that blends superbly with the temple's natural surrounds and striking dry landscaped (sand) garden. (see more on page 16; www.shokoku-ji. jp; fee ¥500).

Ginkaku-ji only takes about 30–45 minutes to fully take in, and after that it's time to start walking. Beginning about 150 meters (490 feet) west of the entrance to Ginkaku-ji you can stroll south along the **Philosopher's Path**, a walkway alongside a partly cherry blossom-lined canal (in bloom late March to early April) that takes its name from a Meiji-era

The Philosopher's Path

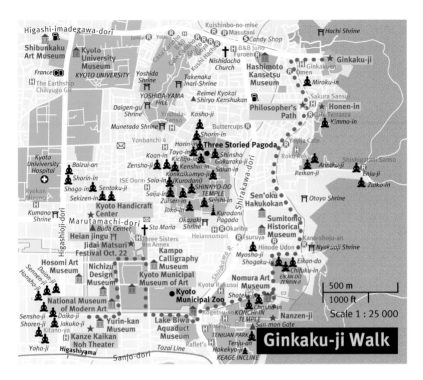

Higashi-imadegawa-dori
Shibunkaku Art Museum
Kyoto University Museum
KYOTO UNIVERSITY
France
The Earthship Chikyugo GH
Junsai
Yata
Casa Gaishoku
Café Gaishoku
Kuishinbo-no-mise
Masutani
Candy Shop
Nishidacho Church
Furoen
Hashimoto Kansetsu Museum
B&B Juno
Ginkakuen
Omen
Ginkaku-ji
Miroku-in
Yoshida Shrine
Takenaka Inari-Shrine
YOSHIDA-YAMA HILL
Reimei Kyokai Shiryo Kenshukan
Sakura Sansui
Daigen-gu Shrine
Yoshida-Sanso
Kosho-ji
Philosopher's Path
Honen-in
Café Terrazza
Kimmo-in
Munetada Shrine
Buttercups
Shorin-in
Yonbanchi 4
Horin-in
Three Storied Pagoda
Yojija Cafe
Kyoto Univiversity Hospital
Baizui-an
Koan-in
Toyo-in
Kichijo-in
Shinsho
Gokuraku-ji
Roku Roku
Zensho-ji
Kenshin-in
Saiun-in
Anraku-ji
Shishigatani Sanso
Shorin-in
ISE Dorm
Konkaikomyo-ji
Reikan-ji
Enju-ji
Shogo-in
Saio-in (Kurodani)
SHINNYO-DO TEMPLE
Saiju-in
Zuiko-in
Ryokan Mizuno
Sentoku-ji
Saiju-in
Sekizen-in
Zulsen-in
Joko-in
Seishi-in
Sen'oku Hakukokan
Otoyo Shrine
Kumano Shrine
Kyoto Handicraft Center
Marutamachi-dori
Budo Center
Sta Maria
Okazaki Shrine
Kurodani Pagoda
Okariba
Sumitomo Historical Museum
Heian jingu
Jidai Matsuri Festival Oct. 22
Three Sisters Inn Annex
Heiannomori
Tsuruya
Kano-shoju-an
Nyakuoji Shrine
Kampo Calligraphy Museum
Myosho-ji
Hinode Udon
Hosomi Art Museum
Nichizu Design Museum
Kyoto Municipal Museum of Art
Shogaku-ji
Eikan-do
Chifuku-in
EIKAN-DO ZENRIN-JI
Sennen-ji
Deon-in
Honshu-ji
National Museum of Modern Art
Kyoto Municipal Zoo
Kyoto Rakusui
Nomura Art Museum
Shoteki-in
Chosho-in
Sensho-ji
Daiko-ji
Shoren-ji
Jakuko-ji
Kitano-ya
Yurin-kan Museum
Lake Biwa Aquaduct Museum
Kogetsu-so
KONCHI-IN TEMPLE
Nanzen-ji
San-mon Gate
Yoho-ji
Kanze Kaikan Noh Theater
Higashiyama
Tozai Line
Raflet's
TENJUAN PARK
Tenju-an
Hokekyo-ji
KEAGE INCLINE
Sanjo-dori

Hachi Shrine

500 m
1000 ft
Scale 1 : 25 000

Ginkaku-ji Walk

philosopher called Kitaro Nishida who would stroll the path to clear his mind for contemplation. Besides being a very calming place to walk, there are several good spots on the way to stop by. If you are hungry, **Omen** (page 64), a block east of the path about 75 meters (245 feet) south from its start, specializes in *udon* noodles, while a few minutes down the path is the small and peaceful **Honen-in** (www.honen-in.jp), which is arguably one of Kyoto's most unheralded, yet prettiest and atmospheric temples—its moss-covered gateway leads to an equally mossy garden which includes a picturesque stone bridge that crosses the temple's pond. Better yet, it's free. You only have to pay (for full access) in the first half of April and the first week of November, when the usually off-limits main hall is open to the public to coin-cide with blooming camellias and autumnal colors, respectively.

Several hundred meters further down the pathway south of Honen-in comes another potential place for rest and a snack, **Yojiya Café** (yojiyacafe.com/store/ginkakuji), which serves green tea and

Honen-in

The Sanmon gate at Nanzen-ji Temple

traditional sweets in *tatami*-matted rooms with views over a small landscaped garden. Another half a kilometer south and the path then reaches the Nanzenji area, where you have a choice to make: head west for about 10 minutes for Heian Jingu and the museums and stores in its vicinity or, before that, do a detour south (about a 10-minute walk) to explore the sprawling **Nanzen-ji Temple** complex (http://nanzenji.com), the head temple of the Rinzai school of Zen Buddhism. It's a detour worth taking, because at Nanzen-ji

Temple you'll be visiting a relic from the 13th century, where the highlights include the mighty Sanmon gateway and its pretty, second-story viewing deck, as well as a dry landscape garden (by the main hall, or Hojo) designed by famed early Edo-era landscape gardener Kobori Enshu. If you do take the detour, plan for an additional 90 minutes of walking and looking, before back tracking and moving on to Heian Jingu.

By Kyoto's ancient standards, **Heian Jingu** is very much a newbie. The vivid orange, green and white shrine was only built in 1895 to mark the 1,100th anniversary of Kyoto's foundation. It was, however, constructed with the past very much in mind. The shrine (open sunrise to sunset, with extended hours for special events; www.heianjingu.or.jp; ¥600) is dedicated to two emperors, Kammu (737–806) and Komei (1831–66), the first and last emperors to reign from Kyoto. Design wise many of the buildings are replicas of Kyoto's first imperial palace, which Kammu, Japan's 50th emperor,

Heian Jingu

The gardens at Heian Jingu

would have called home when it was finished in 794. The shrine's gardens, which for many are Heian Jingu's stand-out feature, are also Heian era (794–1185) in style.

Covering a total area of 33,000m² (8 acres), the garden is split into four sections, each distinct in its own right. The Nishi Shin'en (west garden) is centered on a pond that comes to life with irises in early summer. The Minami Shin'en (south garden), which was apparently built for aristocratic garden parties during which guests would use the natural surrounds to compose poetry, is pink with cherry blossoms in spring, before azaleas come in summer and bush clover takes over on autumn. The Naka Shin'en (central garden) and Higashi Shin'en (east garden) are just as impressive.

If you can, visit on October 22 for the Jidai Matsuri (page 77), when the shrine slips back in time with a 2,000-strong procession of people in attire from the different eras that spanned Kyoto's impe-rial years. If you can't, don't worry, a visit to Heian Jingu is well worth it at any time

of the year. And after Heian Jingu, there are quite a few other sights very nearby to check out. Across from the park to the shrine's south (Okazaki-koen) are three museums worth an hour or two: the **National Museum of Modern Art** (page 81), **Kyoto Museum of Traditional Crafts** (aka Fureiaikan, page 80) and **Kyoto Municipal Museum of Art**. Another block south of that is the **Kanze Kaikan** noh theater (page 67), one of Kyoto's top venues for *noh* performances. Just as good is the **Kyoto Handicraft Center** (page 72) immediately over the road from Heian Jingu's northern end, which with a great range of crafts and other local goods is arguably Kyoto's best one-stop souvenir shop.

Main sights Ginkaku-ji, Honen-in, Philosopher's Path, Heian Jingu, Okazakai-koen and surrounding museums and stores. **Time Required** Half a day is enough. **Getting There** From Kyoto Station take City Bus #5, #17 or #100 to the Ginkakuji-mae bus stop (35 minutes). **Where to Eat** Try Omen (page 64) near Ginkaku-ji for lunchtime noodles or Yojiya (page 37) for tea and sweets. For dinner, check out the listings in the Best Restaurants section.

ARASHIYAMA
Scenic walks and temple cuisine at Kyoto's western edge

See pull-out map N16; E9

Togetsukyo Bridge

With an iconic bamboo grove, many historic temples, and lovely natural scenery, the Arashiyama district in western Kyoto should definitely be on your list of outings. Several stations serve the Arashiyama area but it is Arashiyama Station on the Randen Line that offers up the best start to a walk around the area, thanks to a recent redevelopment that has seen the installation of a grove of 600 poles filled with yuzen *kimono* fabric. The **Kimono Forest**, as it called, is especially nice when illuminated at

night, but even by day it is hard not to linger and study the fabric patterns before heading out of the station.

Once out of the station, a walk around Arashiyama follows a well-worn, but interesting route that (for Japanese tourists at least) starts with a brief detour across the Oi River to check out the oft-photographed **Togetsukyo (moon**

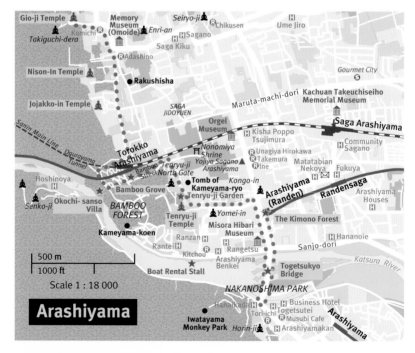

Arashiyama

crossing) **Bridge,** which stretches 150 meters (490 feet) across the river and mixes with the spring cherry blossom and autumnal colors that accent the river banks to create some of Kyoto's prettiest seasonal sights. As with the Kimono Forest, you could easily linger by the river for a while, as it makes a lovely spot for a picnic and on the opposite side there are food stalls along with a dozen or so cafes and restaurants to grab coffee or a tasty bowl of noodles.

Tenryu-ji in fall

Leaving the river behind and backtrack to the station before heading west for a few hundred meters, the next highlight of Arashiyama is **Tenryu-ji** temple **(www. tenryuji.com/en)**, built in the 1300s on the site of a villa that had belonged to the emperor Go-Daigo. While the architecture of the temple's buildings is worthy of note, the main appeal of Tenryu-ji is the 14th-century landscape garden, which uses the concept of "borrowed scenery", in which the surrounding hills form the garden's natural backdrop. Like so many temple gardens, it is especially impressive when the cherry blossoms of spring and earthy tones of fall accent it. Not that Tenryu-ji is all about looking. If you are getting hungry and are interested in some subtle local flavors, the temple also

Tenryu-ji's famous "borrowed scenery" garden

The bamboo grove in Arashiyama

houses a restaurant (**Shigetsu**; daily 11 a.m.–2 p.m.; multi-dish set meals from ¥3,000 to ¥7,000; www.tenryuji.com/en/ shigetsu) that serves dishes using tofu, *yuba* and seasonal vegetables as part of a traditional *shojin-ryori* course, the vegetarian cuisine of Buddhist monks.

Leave Tenryu-ji via its north gate and you'll be at the start of Arashiyama's famous **bamboo grove** (page 15). The combination of the light, which is filtered by the towering bamboo, and the creaking sounds the bamboo makes as it sways gently in the breeze makes for a mesmerizing 15 minutes as you walk through the grove on to the next stop of the tour—the **Okochi-sanso Villa** (9 a.m.–5 p.m.; ¥1,000) to the right at a T-junction about 200 meters (655 feet) into the grove. Once the home of actor Okochi Denjiro (1898–1962), the villa whispers "a-list" at every turn, from the *wabi-sabi* simplicity and elegance of Denjiro's former residence to the meandering landscaped garden that offers up a succession of seasonally changing views and at times sprawling vistas. And although ¥1,000 seems steep, bear in mind that admission includes a ticket for a cup of green tea and a Japanese sweet in a traditional teahouse.

After the villa, you could continue north of the bamboo grove to see the old townhouses and thatched farmhouses of the **Saga Toriimoto** area or, if you are in need of more temples, search out some of the area's other gems in the shape of **Gio-ji** and **Jojakko-ji**. The best way to finish the trip, however, is to head back to Arashiyama Station and pop your feet in the station's hot-spring footbaths to soothe away the day's walking, ideally late enough in the day for the surrounding Kimono Forest to be gently illuminated. Maybe even try a little retail therapy at the shops in and immediately around the station; places like **Kurochiku** for traditional paper and fabric crafts (www.kurochiku.co.jp), Japanese cosmetics at **Momohada** (momohada.com) or **Kyo no Otsukaimon** (www.kyonootsukaimon.net) for a range of modern and traditional crafts and souvenirs. If you are in need of a snack, the station also has a variety of traditional sweet shops—a well-earned sugar rush after all the walking.

Okochi-sanso Villa

Arashiyama Boat Tours

If the weather is good and you want to add a few hours to take in some nature and make Arashiyama a full day out, consider starting the day with a boat tour. From JR Arashiyama Station, the boat tour option starts with a 25-minute ride to Kameoka on the Sagano Scenic Railway, a rural route that winds alongside the wooded river, providing some beautiful, rugged scenery. At Kameoka, after a 10-minute walk to the river, you can then catch one of the 20-seater punts back down the river to Arashiyama, a 90-minute trip that originated in the early 1600s when the river was opened for industrial transportation, but now is purely for tourists. Besides interesting rock formations and several rapids, the ravine provides stunning seasonal views that include not just the rich colors of autumn, but cherry blossoms in spring and occasionally a smattering of snow in January or February.

Main sights The scenery of the Oi River and Togetsukyo Bridge, Tenryu-ji, Kimono Forest, bamboo groves, Okochi-sanso Villa, and the chance for some shopping and a relaxing foot bath. **Time Required** Half a day is enough. **Getting There** Take the Randen (Keifuku) Arashiyama Line, which starts at Shijo-Omiya in central Kyoto, to Arashiyama Station. **Where to Eat** There are a variety of options near Arashiyama Station, but for something very Zen consider a multi-dish Buddhist lunch at Tenryu-ji (page 42). You can also have a cup of green tea with sweets at the Okochi-sanso Villa (page 42). **Insider Tip** If you don't fancy doing Arashiyama on foot, there are **rental bicycles** at the station. The cheapest option, Ranbura, has 30 bikes in all (so you can't be guaranteed to get one), most of which are three-geared and some that are electric. The cost is just ¥150 for a full day and it is located just beyond the railway crossing that the trains go over as they slow down into the station. Alternatively, you could opt for a rickshaw ride around the area (page 87). **Arashiyama boat tours fees and times** Adults ¥3,900, under-12s ¥2,500. Boats leave at least hourly on weekdays (on the hour) from 9 a.m.–2 p.m., but more frequently on weekends. No boats during the Japanese New Year vacation. More details available at the tourist office in Kyoto Station.

Kyoto Station

See pull-out map K11–L12; Q17–R19

When you step off the *shinkansen* (bullet train) at Kyoto expecting to be met by *geisha*s and gardens, the cavernous contemporary design of **Kyoto Station** can almost be a disappointment. Designed by Hiroshi Hara and unveiled in 1997, for many Kyotoites to have the ancient capital represented by something many deemed a modern eyesore was a cultural abomination. Opinion is still split, but whatever you feel about it, Kyoto Station will be a key hub when exploring the city. It's from here that you'll often be catching buses to areas covered in other sections of this book; it's home to a very helpful tourist information center (page 92); it's where you can pick up the handy one-day bus pass, not to mention grab an easy lunch or dinner in the malls under and streets around the station. Kyoto Station is also where you will need to catch a train if you head on to Nara (page 48), or if you want to explore southern Kyoto as outlined in this section.

That journey south starts with a quick one-stop jaunt on the JR Nara Line from Kyoto Station to Tofuku-ji Station, from where it's just a ten-minute walk to the temple complex of the same name.

Tofuku-ji Temple

Tofuku-ji temple (www.tofukiji.jp) has a lot going for it; not only is it so centrally located and relatively uncrowded compared to many other Kyoto sights, it reveals picturesque scenes like its famous 15th-century Zen-style gate and the wooden **Tsuten-kyo bridge**, which is especially beautiful when engulfed in autumn foliage. More than anything, however, Tofuku-ji is also home to arguably Kyoto's finest modern gardens. Rich in traditional Zen conceptualism that's blended with modern accents, the gardens in question were built in 1939 by landscape gardener Mirei Shigemori, who arranged them in small, yet distinct quarters around the temple's main hall (the Hojo).

Mirei's southern quadrant, set in front of the main hall, features groupings of rocks and mossy "mountains" on a raked sand base to create a Zen archipelago. The northern garden is like a checkers board of moss and paving tiles. The eastern garden uses cylindrical stones arranged on a lush mossy carpet to depict the Ursa Major (Great Bear) constellation.

Fushimi Inari Shrine's *torii* gateways

And the western garden has trimmed azalea-shrubs dividing squares of moss and sand in the Chinese *seiden* style.

From Tofuku-ji Station, one more stop south on the Nara Line is Inari Station, and the oft-photographed **Fushimi Inari Shrine**. Dating to the early 700s, the shrine is known for its 10,000 or so vermilion *torii* gateways, which cover four kilometers (two and a half miles) of winding pathways leading up and around wooded mountains—creating one of Kyoto's most distinctive sights and atmospheric walks. The shrine itself is covered in more detail on page 13, but it isn't the only reason to stop off at Fushimi—thanks to the quality of its water, the area is also Kyoto's most famous *sake* brewing district. If *sake* interests you, after Fushimi Inari Shrine, hop on the Keihan Line at Fushimi Inari Station (200 meters/655 feet north of the Nara Line's Inari Station) and head ten minutes south to Chushojima Station to the **Gekkeikan Okura Sake Museum** (¥300, 9.30 a.m.–4.30 p.m., www.gekkeikan.co.jp/english/products/museum). Run by major *sake* brewer Gekkeikan, which was founded in Fushimi in 1637, the museum offers a detailed look at the history of *sake* brewing in Fushimi, the tools used over the years, and the processes involved, but it also has a mini

Tofuku-ji's modern garden

Sake barrels

brewery on site that visitors can peer into and has a shop and tasting area where you can sample various *sake* styles. With a little planning you can also add a full *sake* brewery tour to your time in Fushimi with a visit to the historic **Yamamoto Honke brewery**, which has been operating in Fushimi since 1667. It's about 150 meters (490 feet) north of the museum, but the English-language brewery tour needs to be booked at least a week in advance: www.kyotosake.com.

Even further south on the Nara Line (or on the Keihan-Uji Line from

Chushojima, if you visit the *sake* museum in Fushimi), about 30 minutes from Kyoto Station on non-express services, lies **Uji,** a town in part known for its tea fields and the highly-valued leaves they produce, in part for being the site of one of the country's most recognizable temples—**Byodo-in Temple** (www.byodoin.or.jp), the temple depicted on the back of the 10-yen coin. It takes 10 to 15 minutes to walk to Byodo-in Temple along a well signed route, all the way passing places selling tea and variations on a theme: green tea chocolates, green tea ice cream, green tea cakes, and even green tea liquors and spirits. It's a pleasant stroll, too, especially once you reach the older, wooden building-lined Byodo-in Omotesando street just before the temple.

As for the temple itself, like many temples in and around Kyoto, Byodo-in Temple was once an aristocratic villa, one of many that made Uji something of an aristocrat's retreat in the early days of

Byodo-in Temple

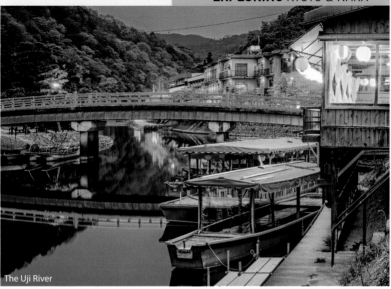
The Uji River

Kyoto's time as capital. In the 11th century, the villa was converted into a temple and a great hall (the Phoenix Hall) was added to house a gilded statue of Amida that remains in situ today in the original hall, whose structure stretches out left and right like a heron extending its wings in flight, about to land on the glistening pond before it. It's a sight well worth the 500 yen admission, even if you are likely to be sharing the view with crowds of selfie stick-wielders trying to get a shot of themselves in front of the hall holding a 10-yen coin. For an extra 300 yen you can also go inside the main temple building—worth it if there isn't a queue, but not if, as is often the case on weekends, you have to wait upwards of an hour.

After Byodo-in Temple, take some time to explore the banks of the nearby **Uji River**, as it's a lovely, peaceful spot with thick woods all about it, and then consider crossing the river to visit the **Tale of Genji Museum**, which is dedicated to the 11th-century book of the same name. The lengthy and influential tale of Heian court intrigue, which follows the life of an imperial prince, was written by female courtier Murasaki Shikibu and is said to be the world's very first novel. Its final ten chapters are set in Uji, which makes it Uji's third claim to fame after its temple and tea.

Main sights The gardens of Tofuku-ji Temple, the sprawling Fushimi Inari Shrine and its thousands of *torii* gateways, Fushimi *sake*, the green tea and legendary Byodo-in Temple in Uji. **Time Required** A full day. **Getting There: Train** Start from Kyoto Station, taking the JR Nara Line to Tofuku-ji Station, then on to Inari Station and finally Uji Station. On the way back to Kyoto from Uji, you can take either the frequent 30-minute local service or one of the twice-hourly express services that take 16 minutes. **Where to Eat** Grab lunch in Uji, but save dinner for when you are back in Kyoto. Byodo-in Omotesando and the street leading to it from the station both have lots of lunchtime options, ranging from cafes to places selling *udon* noodles and soba noodles (some of the latter flavored with green tea), *donburi* (bowls of rice topped with things such as *tempura* or seafood), and the like. Expect to pay between 800 and 1,500 yen. **Insider Tip** If you start the day early and are up for a very long day out, you could head another 30 minutes on from Uji to Nara (page 48) and take in one or two of the main sights there before traveling back to Kyoto. You could also cherry pick a handful of attractions from this day trip and the Nara day trip and combine into one. Of course, if you have the time, schedule to do Nara as an independent day trip or as an overnighter and explore the city properly.

EXPLORING NARA
The ancient birthplace of Japanese civilization

See pull-out map T20–Y22

N ara was Japan's capital from 710 to 794, preceding Kyoto in the role, and is often cited as the place where Japanese civilization evolved—where the culture, religions and social structures that defined what we now think of as "old Japan" firmly took root. By comparison to Kyoto, where the main attractions are spread about a modern city, central Nara almost feels like stepping back in time, or at least stepping into a place where the typically hectic nature of modern Japan takes a back seat to history.

After arriving from Kyoto at **Kintetsu Nara Station**, walk a couple of hundred meters east up the main street and you can literally smell **Nara Park** and its

famous inhabitants—the *shika* (deer), with their unmistakable farmyard mustiness filling the air. The deer are largely tame and will happily descend en mass on anybody with a pack of the 150-yen *shika senbei* (deer crackers) sold by vendors all over the park, but as the warning signs point out with quite comical cartoons, just be aware that every so often one of them bites, charges or head-butts a tourist. You might also want to watch where you are stepping, unless you want to traipse deer dung back to your hotel room.

Nara Park itself is a lovely, sprawling green space in which to simply hang about, and deer aside it's also home to several of Nara's most prominent attractions. Walking east from Kintetsu Nara Station, the first of these you will see (on your right) is the 7th-century **Kofuki-ji Temple** (www.kohfukuji.com), which is known for its 600-year-old five-story pagoda, the original of which was moved here from Kyoto in the early 700s. Anyone with an interest in traditional Asian artwork will want to stop here to

Nara Park

Kofuki-ji Temple

see the 15th-century Token-do hall just north of Kofuku-ji's pagoda, which houses a collection of Buddhist statues that date as far back as the 8th century, before dropping by the modern Kokuhokan hall which is home to Nara's most famed image, a standing statue of the three-headed, six-armed Ashura (one of Buddha's guardians).

Moving on from Kofuku-ji, continuing deeper into Nara Park, comes a very different structure, the Western-style Meiji-era **Nara National Museum** (page 81), which is worth a visit for its extensive collection of Japanese and other Asian arts and artifacts. From the museum area, if you keep going east to the far end of the park, you'd next be at the historic **Kasuga Shrine** (Kasuga Taisha; www.kasugataisha.or.jp). First built in 786, Kasuga is known for its rows of stone lanterns on the approach to the main shrine, which are then replaced by an equally impressive collection of 3,000 or so bronze lanterns hanging within the shrine. Arguably more interesting, however, is the 250-ha (620-acre) **Kasugayama Primeval Forest** and its abundance of insect and birdlife that

stretches out behind the shrine's grounds. One good reason other than history to make the 10-minute walk to this part of the park is that en route there are a couple of good places to stop for lunch—you could stop by the charmingly thatched **Mizutani-chaya** (www.mizuyachaya.com) for tea, sweets or a simple bowl of noodles, or just beyond that try **La Case** (quicheteria-lecase.com), which

Kasuga Shrine

The Daibutsu at Todai-ji Temple

specializes in quiche but also does a range of French desserts and coffee.

Head instead (or next) to the northern part of the park, passing rows of souvenir stores that are probably best ignored in favor of the shops in Nara-machi later in this section, and the towering Nandai-mon gateway to **Todai-ji Temple** (www.todaiji.or.jp) soon looms into view. Part of the Nara's collective World Heritage designation, which was granted in 1998, Todai-ji Temple is undoubtedly one of the major highlights of any visit to Nara. Founded in 745 by the Emperor Shomu at such a cost that it is said the Imperial court nearly went bankrupt during the 15 years it took to complete, the complex includes one of the largest wooden buildings in the world in the shape of the 57-meter (185-foot) long and 50-m (165-foot) wide Daibutsu-en hall, which was built to house a 15-meter (50-foot) tall bronze statue of Buddha (Japan's largest bronze image). Weighing in at an impressive 500 tons, the partially remodeled Daibutsu of Nara hasn't had the easiest of times since it was unveiled in 752, having had its (now replaced) head knocked off in a 9th-century earthquake, his hands melted twice in fires in the 12th and 16th centuries, and his gilding blackened with age, but it is still a magnificent sight. While you are there, take

the time to walk around the whole of the hall, as there are some interesting features that includes a hole in one of the pillars behind the Daibutsu that, if legend is correct, offers immediate enlightenment to anyone who can crawl through it.

For a break from the museums, temples and shrines, from Todai-ji Temple you can backtrack to Kintetsu Nara Station on foot in 10 to 15 minutes (or take the yellow bus route from the bus stop south of Todai-ji Temple—stop N7—to bus stop N3) and wander the area to the south of the station. You can start with the covered **Higashi-muki** mall that runs southward from the station and then leads on to the uncovered **Mochiiodono shopping street**, both of which are home to a collection of places to grab a quick bite to eat and shop (page 73), before reaching the Nara-machi area.

Full of traditional wooden houses and narrow alleys, **Nara-machi** is a charming old district to explore—partly just because of the calm, quiet ambience, but mainly because so many of the historic buildings hold something worth delving into, be that one off many quaint cafes or a craft shop. For lunch or dinner, you could stop by **Harishin** (page 65) here for an affordable, but beautifully presented mixture of *sashimi*, *tempura* and other Japanese delicacies, or you could check out stores such as the 400-year-old **Kobaien** and its calligraphy ink stinks, the multi-store **Kai** (www.kai.st) which brings together a variety of artisans, or **Yu Nakagawa** and its sun-bleached linens that are used to make a variety of clothing, apparel and interior goods. The beauty of Nara-machi is that if you give the area a couple of leisurely hours of your time, you will unearth far more than the listings above.

If you wanted more temples, consider ending the day by visiting the magnificent

Horyu-ji Temple

Horyu-ji Temple, which is a 12-minute jaunt to Horyu-ji Station on the Yamatoji Line from JR Nara Station. You could even consider adding a night in Nara and doing Horyu-ji Temple on day two, before heading back to Kyoto via Uji and Fushimi (see the day trip on page 44 for the latter two). Covered in more detail on page 19, Horyu-ji Temple was first built in the early 600s and served as an important base for Buddhism's early and rapid expansion in Japan, and one of its main attractions today is its collection of treasures dating back to that period. It's also home to some striking structures, most notably a five-story pagoda that is said to be one of the oldest buildings in the world, with the wood used for its construction having been dated as being cut in 594. Just be warned that Horyu-ji Temple isn't cheap—it's ¥1,500. From there, it's easy to head back to Nara or Kyoto on JR Lines (Yamatoji Line to Nara, then Nara Line to Kyoto).

Main sights Several World Heritage-designated temples and shrines, Nara Park and its semi-tame deer, the old Nara-machi district and its craft stores, Nara National Museum. **Time Required** A full day. If you want to stay overnight, check out the Nara accommodation options and advice in Chapter 3 (page 59). **Getting There** From Kyoto Station take either the JR Nara Line or the Kintetsu Line to JR Nara Station or Kintetsu Nara Station, respectively. The two stations are about a 10-minute walk apart, but yellow city buses also run between the two on a loop route that also goes to Nara-machi (N-13 Tanaka-cho bus stop), Nara Park and Todai-ji (stops N-8 to N-6), and Kofuku-ji (stop N-3). **Where to Eat** There are a couple of suggestions for a memorable dinner on page 65, while the Nara-machi area (page 50) is home to some casual options with a bit of character and the malls (page 73) running south of Kintetsu Nara Station have affordable options that range from local noodles and curry to Indian and Italian. **Insider Tip** It's a very acquired taste, but if you ask a Japanese friend what food they most associate with Nara, they will very likely say, "Narazuke". These deep-brown pickles are either *daikon* (the large white Japanese radish), *uri* (a kind of bitter gourd) or cucumber that have have been soaked in *sake* lees for months (even years) and have taken on a pungent flavor that is often accompanied with a sherry-like kick. Most of the souvenir shops sell them and many will have free samples you can try.

DAY TRIP TO OSAKA
A whirlwind visit to Japan's second largest city

Forty kilometers (25 miles) west of Kyoto and with a population of just under 11 million, Osaka is the Kansai region's modern yin to Kyoto and Nara's ancient yang. Japan's bustling second city has long been a commercial powerhouse, even surpassing Tokyo until the Meiji era, but it's also known among Japanese for many other things, both good and bad—the best comedians are said to be Osakan, as are the most successful *yakuza* groups; Osakans have a reputation for being more direct, open, and warmer than the typical Japanese (and especially stereotypically reserved Kyotoites), and their distinctive dialect (called Osaka-ben) can certainly be more colorful and earthy than standard Japanese. As a

break from Kyoto and Nara's past, a day trip to Osaka provides an energetic and invigorating change of pace and scenery.

To explore the city, you could start with its roots and **Osaka Castle** (www.osaka-castle.net; 9 a.m.–5 p.m.; ¥600; see Getting There for directions). First built by Toyotomi Hideyoshi in 1585, but rebuilt several times since, the current eight-story structure dates from 1931 and dominates the skyline from a hilltop perch that gives great views across the city. Better still is what's inside; several floors of feudal artifacts that include swords and armor, as well as painted screens and scrolls. And while in the area, half a kilometer northwest of the castle, another historic stop could be the 10th-century **Tenmangu Shrine**, which is dedicated to Sugawara no Michizane, Japan's patron saint of scholars. If you were to come here on the 5th, 10th or 25th of any month you would see students visiting to pray for success with their studies (and exam results). If you were lucky enough to be here on July 24th and 25th, you'd get to see Tenmangu come alive with fireworks, a procession of floats, and lantern-lit boats plying the nearby canal as part of the shrine's annual festival.

Heading southwest of the castle about 1.5 kilometers/one mile (near either Namba, Nipponbashi or Ebisucho stations) comes a very different experience, with the **DenDen Town shopping district** and its home electronics, gaming and *manga/anime* stores. Very much Osaka's answer to Tokyo's Akihabara district—Japan's *otaku* (geek) center—the two long streets that make up DenDen throw up an interesting selection of stores that can easily soak up a couple of hours for browsing. For *anime* and *manga* fans, Animate (www.animate.co.jp) in particular is a must-visit for its collection of geeky goods and comics, while the

Osaka Castle

branches of Super Potato (www.superpo-tato.com) in the area are packed with retro video games, if that's your thing. From the southern end of DenDen, walking a few hundred meters east of Ebisucho Station, is another change of pace (if you haven't had enough temples in Kyoto and Nara already) at **Shitenno-ji** temple (www.shitennoji.or.jp). Although mostly a modern rebuild, Shitenno-ji's stone *torii* gateway, which is unusual to see in a temple, dates to the 1200s. The temple itself was founded in 593 by Prince Shotoku (who was also behind the ancient temples of Nara, page 48), making it the oldest temple in the country.

From the north end of DenDen (near Nippombashi Station), Namba Station is only a few hundred meters west. Here you'll find more shopping in places like the large Marui department store and Bic Camera home electronics store, but more interesting is the **Dotombori** area that begins just north of Namba. This crowded, neon-lit area—often referred to as Osaka's main entertainment district — feels like the city's heartbeat.

Dotombori is the best place to end the day with a drink or dinner, and in particular it has plenty of places to try *okonomiyaki*, a classic of Osaka that is hard to translate, but could fairly be described as a kind of pancake. A mix of shredded cabbage and batter to which meat or seafood is added along with anything from *kimchee* to cheese, *okonomiyaki* is then cooked (usually by diners themselves) on hot plates built into each table. You then top it with a thick brown sauce, sprinkle it with dried seaweed and dried *bonito* flakes (and maybe add some mayo), and it is one of the finest and most enjoyable examples of what the Japanese call *b-kyu gurume* (lit. b-grade gourmet food; meaning cheap, but delicious foods that also include *ramen* and *gyoza*). One that's easy to find and

Dotombori

justifies its fame among *okonomiyaki* places is **Mizuno** (daily 11 a.m.–10 p.m.; about ¥1,500 without drinks), about 50 meters (165 feet) south of a sub-branch of **Kani Doraku** (a crab restaurant with a big crab hanging off the building). But there are so many others all over Osaka you can easily find somewhere else. And as a good rule, anything with a queue will be worth waiting for. As for Kani Doraku (douraku.co.jp; courses from ¥6,000), any of their three restaurants in Dotombori (including the original) are worth queuing for, too, if you like the idea of set courses that include crab *shabu shabu* (hotpot), crab *sashimi*, and grilled crab.

Main sights Osaka Castle, the Dotombori entertainment district, the electronic stores of DenDen town, Tenmangu Shrine, and Shitenno-ji temple. **Time Required** A full day. **Getting There** From Kyoto Station don't make the mistake of wasting money on the *shinkansen* for what's still a fairly short trip on standard JR Lines. To start at Osaka Castle (as detailed above), take the JR Tokaido-Sanyo Line to Osaka Station and from there transfer to the JR Osaka Loop Line for Osakajo-koen Station. It'll cost ¥800 and take about 45 minutes. **Where to Eat** The Dotombori area is packed with places to eat and drink, whether you want local flavors or something more familiar from home. See the suggestions in the text for trying the classic local dish *okonomiyaki*. **Insider Tip** Also in Osaka (although out of the way by the western waterfront) is Universal Studios Japan, a 57-hectare (140-acre) site that mimics much of the US original, but also has some Japan-only attractions. See more about this in the Kid-friendly Attractions section on page 75. It's difficult to incorporate USJ into a day out that also includes central Osaka, but it is a good alternative for a break from Kyoto.

CHAPTER 3
AUTHOR'S RECOMMENDATIONS

From the best places to stay to unforgettable cultural experiences, fine *kyo-ryori* restaurants to scenic mountainside strolls, and souvenir hunting spots to kid-friendly attractions and much, much more, here are our author's picks for the best of the best in Kyoto and Nara.

Best Accommodations

Gion Kinpyo (Machiya Townhouse)
Hiiragiya Ryokan
Koke-an (Machiya Townhouse)
Matsubaya Ryokan
Shunkoin Temple
First Cabin
Hotel Mume
Hyatt Regency Kyoto
The Screen
Ritz-Carlton Kyoto
Nara Hotel
Ryokan Seikanso

Best Restaurants

Kaiseki at Minokou
Modern Fusion at Giro Giro Hitoshina
Home-style Cooking at Kokoroya
Ramen at Ippudo
Vegetarian Cuisine at Ikkyu-an
Kaitenzushi at Musashi
Tempura at Yoshikawa
Udon Noodles at Omen
Grilled Eel at Matsuno
Harishin
Tsukihitei

Nightspots & Entertainment

Gion Corner Theater
Geisha Shows
Kanze Kaikan
Minami-za
Craft Beer at Bungalow
Drinks and Art at Tranq Room
Try an Izakaya
Yoramu Sake Bar
Live Music at Taku Taku or
    Greenwich House
Clubbing at Lab Tribe and Metro

Best Shopping

Chirimen Fabrics at Manekinekonote
Flea Market at To-ji temple
Kimono and Fabrics at Mimuro
Kiyomizu Pottery at Asahido
Kyoto Handicraft Center
Japanese Teas at Fukujuen
Shopping for Antiques
Mochiinodo Center Gai
The Nara-machi Area

Kid-friendly Attractions

Umekoji Train Museum
Kyoto Aquarium
Kyoto International Manga Museum
TOEI Studio Park
Universal Studios in Osaka

Festivals & Events

Cherry Blossom Viewing
Aoi Matsuri
Gion Matsuri
Daimon-ji Gozan Fire Festival
Jidai Matsuri

Best Cultural Experiences

Try the Tea Ceremony
Zen Meditation
Cooking Classes and Tours
Other Cultural Classes

Best Galleries & Museums

Kyoto National Museum
Kyoto Museum of Traditional Crafts
Ii Museum
Kyoto Garden of Fine Arts
National Museum of Modern Art
Nara National Museum

BEST ACCOMMODATION

More than just a place to rest your head

Be it traditional Japanese inn (*ryokan*) or 100-year-old *machiya* townhouse, five-star modern luxury or fashionable boutique hotel, Kyoto has a range of accommodation to suit all tastes and needs. Here are the best of Kyoto's modern and traditional accommodation options, as well as some tips on budget options and booking sites.

TRADITIONAL ACCOMMODATIONS

Gion Kinpyo (Machiya Townhouse)

A night at a *ryokan* is a wonderful experience, but for a few days in Kyoto so is basing yourself in an old townhouse like the charming Gion Kinpyo. Once a small *sake* brewery, this Edo-era building features dark timbers and high vaulted ceilings, which with the old *sake* brewing paraphernalia that dots the place provides frequent reminders that you are staying somewhere full of history. Being a Kyo-machiya, no meals are included, which makes a stay here more affordable than a high-end *ryokan* (where meals are almost always included) and means you are free to explore Kyoto's restaurants in the nearby Gion, Kawaramachi and Shijo-dori areas; although if you did want to eat in the *machiya*, the friendly English-speaking family that owns it can have local restaurants deliver. To round things off, there's also a scented *hinoki* bath on the second floor, which overlooks a small *tsuboniwa* courtyard garden. *www.kinpyo.jp. From ¥13,000 per person, but book well in advance in peak seasons.*

Hiiragiya Ryokan

1968 Nobel Prize for Literature winner

Gion Kinpyo

Hiiragiya Ryokan

Yasunari Kawabata, a regular at the 200-year-old Hiiragiya, once said, "It is here, at Hiiragiya, that I wistfully recall that sense of tranquility that belonged to old Japan." Having stayed here, I doubt that atmosphere has changed at all since Kawabata's days, nor in earlier years when the likes of Elizabeth Taylor and Charlie Chaplin discovered old Kyoto here. Not that the Hiiragiya is a museum. With a choice of bright, newly created rooms that employ traditional craftsmanship and *ryokan* design or darker historic rooms that mostly date to the *ryokan*'s opening, and which (depending on the room) have features such as Edo-era painted screen doors and private ornamental gardens, the Hiiragiya offers a nice variety of rooms. Whichever room type you opt for, everything else that comes with the Hiiragiya experience is equally magical—sublime *kaiseki* cuisine, impeccable yet warm service and an atmosphere that is as calming as a soak in the *ryokan*'s hot spring baths. *www.hiiragiya.co.jp. Per person rates with two meals start from around ¥30,000 but can go much higher.*

Koke-an (Machiya Townhouse)

Renting out an old *machiya* townhouse like Koke-an offers a private, atmospheric and at times affordable alternative to staying in a hotel, and can be a great option for families or anyone traveling in a group. In Koke-an's case, the combination of two connected old buildings tucked down a quite side alley means it can sleep 4 to 6 people. And even though it is a peaceful location, complete with a very small mossy garden from which the house takes its name (*koke* means moss), its location on the corner of Sanjo-dori puts it just two minutes from the subway system. Depending on the season, Koke-an costs ¥22,000 to ¥28,000 per night for a group of 3–4 people, with each additional person costing ¥2,000 extra, while the full kitchen can also help cut costs by self-catering. *Can be booked through www.kyotomachiyastay.com, who have seven other machiya in Kyoto, ranging from intimate machiya aimed at couples, such as its Shirakawa Cottage, to larger family-friendly options.*

Matsubaya Ryokan

The Matsubaya is traditional accommodation striped of the frills to provide a *ryokan* experience for travelers on a budget. Unlike most *ryokan*, there is no communal *onsen* (bath) and no dinners are served here, but the rooms have everything *ryokan* fans would expect—*tatami* mat flooring, sliding screen doors, and *futon* at night. Also unlike most *ryokan*, singles start at a bargain ¥4,400 and twins from ¥8,100. The *ryokan*'s largest rooms (¥33,000) will sleep five people, making it a good choice for families, too. And the location is also not to be sniffed at, being just a ten-minute walk from JR Kyoto Station and five minutes from Gojo subway Station. Breakfasts available at an extra cost. *www.matsubayainn.com.*

Shunkoin Temple

Shunkoin Temple

Situated in one of the sub-temples of the Myoshinji temple complex in northwest Kyoto, this peaceful *shukubo* (temple lodging) has eight simple, but well-maintained private rooms (each sleeping 1–3 people) going for just ¥4,500 to ¥6,000 per person. As you might expect for temple accommodation, Shunkoin is no frills, but guests have access to a well-equipped shared kitchen and the rooms all come with air-conditioning, shower, toilet, *futon* and WiFi access. Add to that the hospitality of the English-speaking vice abbot, the Rev. Kawakami, who offers daily meditation sessions, plus Shunkoin's proximity to Ryoan-ji, Kinkaku-ji and other must-see sights, and Shunkoin is a gem. ***www.shunkoin.com.***

KYOTO HOTELS

First Cabin

A capsule hotel with a touch of boutique, First Cabin themes itself on air travel, with business class (measuring 2.5 m² /25 ft²; ¥4,600 per night) and first class

(4.5 m²/50 ft²; ¥5,600 per night) "cabins" that provide a simple, small but smart place to lay your head. The cabins all come with free WiFi access, unexpectedly comfy bed and flat-screen TV, and unlike traditional typically male-only capsule hotels, there is a women-only floor here, too. There is also a lounge area that serves a few simple dishes (such as fried rice) along with beer and soft drinks, so you don't have to hang out just in your cabin. Located by Karasuma Station. ***www.first-cabin.jp.***

Hotel Mume

Located alongside the Shirakawa River in the Gion area, this intimate boutique hotel has seven rooms designed around the classical concept of *ka-cho-fu-getsu* (bird, butterfly, wind, moon). The room décor, which mixes modern design sensibilities with traditional touches such as antique furnishings brought in from all over the globe, has certainly made Mume a unique prospect in Kyoto. Where else in the city will you find rooms mixing golds with dark woods; or with jet black walls offset by red oriental furniture? Rooms from ¥21,000. ***www.hotelmume.com.***

Hyatt Regency Kyoto

Until the Ritz-Carlton (page 59) came along in 2014, the Hyatt Regency was undisputedly the best five-star western-style hotel in Kyoto. The 189 rooms, which were designed by renowned Japanese design house Super Potato, combine the kind of sleek contemporary decor you'd expect in a modern five-star property with traditional design elements such as washi paper fittings and *kimono* fabric headboards. To that, the Hyatt also added highly-rated Japanese, French and Italian restaurants and one of Kyoto's best spas, and the hotel can also boast a

Hyatt Regency Kyoto

fairly handy location—it's one kilometer (about half a mile) east of JR Kyoto Station. Twins and doubles from ¥23,000 per night. *www.kyoto.regency.hyatt.com.*

The Screen

Kyoto doesn't have all that many boutique hotels, but it makes up for the lack of quantity with a high level of quality. The Screen, situated about a five-minute walk from the Imperial Palace Park (page 33), has 13 individually designed luxury rooms that between them incorporate Scandinavian, contemporary Asian and traditional Japanese design sensibilities to very sleek effect. Along with that come a plush champagne lounge, a modern French restaurant, and a café-bar, as well as in summer a rooftop deck with views across the city. Rates per person start at around ¥15,000 per night. If this place is booked up, another boutique option is the Hotel Mume (page 58) in Gion. *www.screen-hotel.jp.*

Ritz-Carlton Kyoto

Depending on which way you look at ultra-luxury hotels, Kyoto has either happily managed to resist their allure where Tokyo hasn't, or the city has long been fairly lacking in the international luxury department. The 134-room Ritz-Carlton, which opened in a low rectangular building along the Kamogawa River in February 2014, has turned that on its head with features that include suites complete with gardens with moon-viewing decks, an Espa spa, two fine restaurants (Mizuki serving Japanese cuisine and La Locanda serving Italian) and a sleek mix of modern and traditional Japanese sensibilities combining to create stunning designs throughout. As you'd expect, all that doesn't come cheaply: doubles will set you back at least ¥70,000. *www.ritzcarlton-kyoto.jp.*

STAYING IN NARA

Although many people visit Nara as a day trip while staying in Kyoto, Nara has plenty of good places to stay if you want to add an extra day or two to explore the city. For a wide range of options, check

Nara Hotel

out the section on business hotels and booking sites (page 60). For a couple of our best picks, read on.

Nara Hotel

Opened in 1909, the Nara Hotel is one of Japan's classic Western-influenced hotels. Blending gracefully ageing Japanese and European styles, the old lady of Nara's hotel scene retains something of a regal air. Staying here today, it's not hard to imagine how it would have felt here back in the 1930s, when the likes of Charles Lindbergh or Charlie Chaplin signed the visitors' book. Skipping forward through the decades, it probably changed little by the time Richard Nixon, Audrey Hepburn and Marlon Brando stayed, too. Today, the guestrooms feel spacious by modern Japanese standards, with enough dating to the design to feel quaint but not crumbling. The restaurants, serving fine French and Japanese cuisine, are equally old school in service and style, while the dark wooden bar feels like stepping back into a Western-style Meija-era retreat. The hotel garnishes all that with a great location near Nara Park. Twins from ¥18,800 per room. ***www.narahotel.co.jp.***

Ryokan Seikanso

Located in a former *geisha* house in the older Nara-machi area of Nara, the Seikanso offers budget accommodation with traditional style and service that belies the price. The nine *tatami*-matted rooms here are well maintained and come complete with sliding screen doors, *futon* and all the other traditional *ryokan* touches, while the sculptured garden surrounding the building adds to the old-Japan character. The friendly English speaking owners are another highlight. But, it's the price that caps it: ¥4,320 per adult and ¥2,700 per child (under 12) in rooms that can sleep up to four. The only drawback for some is that the bathing is communal only. ***www.nara-ryokanseikanso.com/en.***

Japanese Business Hotels

For travelers looking for something reasonably priced, but who don't want to stay in youth hostels, Japan's "business hotels" can be a great option. Chains like Toyoko Inn (www.toyoko-inn.com; four centrally located branches in Kyoto) and Dormy Inn (www.hotespa.net; one branch three minutes from Kyoto Station) both have English-language booking websites and offer simple, well-maintained, albeit blandly designed Western-style rooms with free in-room WiFi or LAN. The Dormy Inn even comes with its own communal hot-spring bath. Prices vary by exact location and season, but expect singles to start from ¥5,000. For other budget options, as well as traditional accommodation in places like Nara, try www.japanican.com, the English-language site of Japan's leading travel agency, JTB.

Classic *kaiseki* cuisine is presented like art

BEST RESTAURANTS

Local flavors from home cooked to the sublime

Be it fine multi-course *kaiseki* dinners or simple handmade noodles, Kyoto and Nara deliver the very best of the full range of Japanese cuisine. Below is a selection of the best restaurants representing a variety of Japanese flavors. Within the guided days out in Chapter 2 there are also plenty of other places highlighted where you can grab something to eat or drink. For more, try Inside Kyoto (www.insidekyoto.com/best-restaurants-in-kyoto) for an excellent breakdown of the best places to eat by food type, or pick up a copy of Judith Clancy's equally good *Kyoto Machiya Restaurant Guide*.

Kaiseki at Minokou
Masterful presentation, attentive service,

tranquil setting, and sublime flavors; all things one should expect from the best Japanese restaurants. In Kyoto, many restaurants tick these boxes for *kaiseki-ryori* or *kyo-ryori* (both multi-course meals comprised of numerous small yet immaculately presented and delicately flavored dishes that feature seasonal produce), and Minokou certainly ranks among the best. Located in Gion, the 100-year-old Minokou contains a maze of wooden corridors that on route to connecting private dining rooms occasionally give up glimpses of a manicured garden. Once in your room, you'll find *tatami*-matted flooring and touches of traditional luxury that include heavy lacquerware tables and *ikebana* flower arrangements, which combined with fine food served by waitresses in the most exquisite of *kimono* creates a quintessential Kyoto experience. Lunch *bento* box from ¥3,500, full dinner from ¥15,000. Reservations are essential. If you can't get one, try Inside Kyoto (www.insidekyoto.com/best-restaurants-in-kyoto) for a rundown of other great *kaiseki* options.

A contemporary take on traditional cuisine

A bowl of *ramen*

Modern Fusion at Giro Giro Hitoshina

Kaiseki meets punk. Traditional roots with a very modern anything-goes attitude. When you walk into Giro Giro and notice the chef has patterns dyed into his hair, you know there's something different going on. Like any great *kaiseki* restaurant, the food here is created with high-quality ingredients by highly-skilled chefs, but at Giro Giro there seems to be some kind of mission to bring fine dining to a new audience. The atmosphere is unusually bustling and casual for *kaiseki*; traditional dishes are given inventive re-workings, with the eight-course dinner here combining classic fine Japanese dining ingredients in ways that would leave some traditionalists aghast; the price is remarkable at just ¥3,680 (cash only). The experience is brilliant. Reservations are essential. *www.guiloguilo.com.*

Home-style Cooking at Kokoraya

One of the great things about dining in Kyoto is to explore the hundreds of restaurants located in atmospheric old townhouses (called *machiya*). In Kokoraya's case, the 120-year-old wooden building it calls home is the perfect setting for simple and rustic *obanzai* (home-style) cooking. As the boxes and baskets of vegetables outside suggest, seasonal produce features heavily on the hand-written menu, but so too does grilled fish such as mackerel and meats like local black beef. The menu can be hard to navigate, so it is probably best to opt for one of their set menus (¥2,500 to ¥3,500), and maybe wash it down with one of the *sake* on the menu. *Tel. 075-211-3348. Open 11.30 a.m.–2 p.m. & 6 p.m.–10 p.m. Closed Wednesdays. kokoraya.moss-co-ltd.com/shopdata/ gokoumachi.*

Ramen at Ippudo

Ramen is something of a national obsession in Japan. People will queue for hours for a few moments of frantic noodle slurping at the best *ramen* joints; the chefs that find that magical combination of ideal noodle texture, broth flavor and consistency and topping quality are held in as much regard by *ramen* aficionados as those with Michelin stars. Ippudo, within a minute from Shijo Station (in Nishiki-koji food market), is no exception. Here you can slurp up perfectly springy noodles in a lovely rich soup that come with a generous topping of roast pork and additional side servings (such as *gyoza* dumplings), and still get change from a ¥1,000 note. You'll probably have to queue, unless you come outside of normal meal times, but the queuing will be worth it. *www.ippudo.com/store/kyoto/nishiki. Open daily 10.30 a.m.–3 a.m.*

Vegetarian Cuisine at Ikkyu-an

Shojin-ryori is the term given to the vegetarian cuisine traditionally eaten by monks, and while the thought of eating like a monk might conjure up images of bland bowls of gruel or something equally austere, in the case of *shojin-ryori* at Ikkyu-an, monk food means something very special. Situated just outside the southeast entrance to the Daitoku-ji temple complex (page 23), Ikkyu-an has been in business for centuries, and in that time they have turned temple staples into the vegetarian equivalent of *kaiseki*, with simple tofu and seasonal vegetables transformed into mini gastronomical masterpieces that are taken sat at low tables on *zabuton* cushions with views across a traditional temple garden. Reservations are essential. If you don't want to drop ¥8,000 to ¥15,000 for dinner, try a smaller lunch *bento* in the same setting for ¥4,000.
www.daitokuji-ikkyu.jp.

Kyoto is famed for its tofu

Kaitenzushi at Musashi

Sushi comes in many settings in Japan, from high-end *sushi* bars to low-budget restaurants called *kaitenzushi* (lit. revolving *sushi*) where ready-made *sushi* travels in front of and alongside diners to be plucked up by whoever wants it (and in many places can be made-to-order and delivered via special conveyor belt direct to one's seat). Even if the high end is within your budget, *kaitenzushi* is still a lot of fun. At Musashi, you get the full *kaitenzushi* experience plus the added help of an English menu so you can order things not on the conveyor belt (which is what many people do anyway for everything they eat at *kaitenzushi*). To keep matters simple, most plates, which usually have two pieces of *sushi*, are only ¥140 each. It's also easy to find, being on the northwest corner of the Sanjo-dori/Kawaramachi-dori intersection.
Open daily 11 a.m.–10 p.m.

Kaitenzushi—sushi on a conveyor

Tempura

Unagi-don (grilled eel)

Tempura at Yoshikawa

When done badly, *tempura* is worse than the soggiest of fish and chips. When done well, it's magnificent. Located within a plush *ryokan* called the Yoshikawa Inn, in a beautiful 100-year old building, this *tempura* restaurant falls comfortably into the latter category with the choice of multi-dish courses in a private *tatami* mat room (some with garden views) or sat watching the chefs at a sunken *tempura* counter that seats just 12. With either, the intimate atmosphere is very much "old Kyoto". And this being Kyoto, you don't just get *tempura* here; the indulgent courses also include delicate seasonal *kaiseki* dishes, *sashimi*, grilled fish, tofu dishes, and more. Reservations are essential. Courses run from ¥8,000 to ¥10,000 at counter seating and ¥10,000 to a staggering ¥25,000 in private rooms, but there are also small ¥4,000 lunch servings on a first-come, first-served basis. *www.kyoto-yoshikawa. co.jp. Open daily 11 a.m.–1.30 p.m. and 5 p.m.–8 p.m. (last order).*

Udon Noodles at Omen

Close to Ginkaku-ji (page 36), Omen (meaning "noodles") specializes in hand-made *udon*, a thick wheat noodle that can come with a hot or cold broth and accompaniments such as *tempura*. For lunch, it makes for a simple, cheap, fill-

ing and tasty meal, but at dinner there are options to have the noodles as part of a course of dishes that also include seasonal vegetable side dishes (such as butterbur sprout in a *miso* paste), deep-fried shrimp and *yakitori* (grilled chicken). Even better is that Omen combines a traditional *tatami*-matted setting with the traditional flavors, but still offers an English menu to take the confusion out of ordering. *www.omen.co.jp. Open daily 11 a.m.–9 p.m.*

Grilled Eel at Matsuno

In Japan *unagi* (eel) is said to be good for building stamina in the energy-draining summer months and, if old wives tales are anything to go by, all year round in the bedroom! If the latter is true, then the family-run Matsuno in Gion (page 30) has been Cupid's main man in Kyoto for several generations. The menu here, which blends traditional dishes and the occasional touch of innovation, includes classic char-grilled eel basted in a sweet and rich soy-based sauce that fills the restaurant with a caramel aroma guaranteed to make mouths water. Adding to that, everything is served up in the convivial and traditional surrounds of an old *machiya* townhouse.

www.matsuno-co-com. Open daily 11.30 a.m.–9 p.m.

Dining in Nara

Nara has lots of dining options. For lunch or dinner, you'll find plenty of eateries in the streets around Nara Park, in the Nara-machi area, and in malls and arcades such as Mochiidono Center Gai (see the main Nara section on page 48 for all of these), with options ranging from noodle restaurants and *sushi-ya* to non-Japanese cuisines that will match all budgets. What follows are a couple of top choices for a memorable meal in Nara.

Harishin

Located in the old Nara-machi area (page 50), Harishin gives the option of dining in a *tatami*-matted area with garden views or around a homely hearth. It's a charming traditional setting for sampling their signature *kamitsumichi bento*, which at ¥2,980 is a very good value way to sample excellent Japanese dishes such as tofu, *tempura*, *sashimi*, and seasonal vegetables cooked in a variety of ways. For ¥6,500 they also serve an almost rustic version of *kaiseki* that's also good value. *www.harishin.com. Open 11.30 a.m.–2.30 p.m. and 6 p.m.–8 p.m. (last orders). Closed most Mondays.*

Tsukihitei

This *kaiseki* restaurant located in a century-old *ryokan* comes with the kind of prices that will cause palpations—upwards of ¥10,000 at lunch and ¥15,000-plus at dinner—but if you are keen to break the bank on a special meal in Nara, Tsukihitei is the place to do it. The location for starters couldn't be better for a traditional meal, being situated in forest behind Todai-ji temple (page 50) in a building that oozes old charms. Then there is the art-like multi-dish course, which is changed monthly to utilize seasonal ingredients at their peak. And, as with any good *kaiseki* place, they have got the service down to the most subtle of fine arts. Reservations essential. *www.nara-ryoutei.com/tsukihitei.*

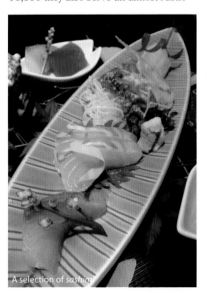

A selection of *sashimi*

Useful restaurant phrases

Do you have an English menu? *Eigo no menyuu ga arimasu ka?* What do you recommend? *O susume wa nan desu ka?* Can I have (some water): *(mizu) o onegai shimasu* Can I have this, please? (said when pointing to something) *Kore o onegai shimasu* It's tasty! *Oishii desu!* Cheers! *Kampai!* Could I have the bill, please? *O-kaikei o onegai shimasu.* Thank you for the meal (said to staff when leaving a restaurant or to people at your table when finishing your meal): *Gochisosama deshita*

NIGHTSPOTS & ENTERTAINMENT

From centuries-old performing arts to new artisanal beers

Whether you want to take in traditional forms of dance and theater, sip on *sake* and craft beer, or need somewhere to head bang the night away, when the temples close their doors for the day, the nightlife in Kyoto (and to a much lesser extent Nara) starts to warm up.

TRADITIONAL THEATER

Gion Corner Theater

For some people a show at **Gion Corner** will feel too touristy, for others the hour-long performance will be a really entertaining primer on traditional forms of artistic expression. The show combines seven types of performances in all: *bunraku* (puppetry), *chado* (tea ceremony), *gagaku* (court music), *ikebana* (flower

Maiko kyomai performance

arranging), *koto* (six-stringed Japanese harp), *kyogen* (comic acting), and *kyomai* (dancing by *maiko*). Five minutes from the Gion bus stop, served from Kyoto Station by City Bus #100 and #206, or ten minutes from Kawaramachi Station. *Open daily (although check online before going as it can vary irregularly) with shows from 6 p.m. and 7 p.m. Adults ¥3,150, cheaper rates for students and children. See: www.kyoto-gioncorner.com.*

Geisha Shows

Gion Corner (see above) isn't the only place to experience a *maiko* or *geisha* performance (although it is the most affordable). If you are in Kyoto at the right time, another option is to take in a seasonal *geisha* show, such as the 145-year-old **Miyako Odori** (www.miyako-odori. jp; tickets ¥2,500 to ¥4,800), which is held daily during April at the **Kaburenjo Theater** and features an extravagant display of *geisha* dancing with a traditional musical accompaniment, plus the option of a pre-show tea ceremony. In May, a similar event at Kaburenjo by a different *geisha* group is the **Kamogawa Odori**. Upping the budget, there are *maiko* dinner nights like those held at the *ryokan* **Gion Hatanaka** (www.gionhatanaka. jp), where for ¥19,000 per person you get a two-hour performance that takes in dance, music, and other traditional arts while eating *kaiseki* cuisine. Heading into super expensive territory, if you want to go for the full-on private *geisha* experience, you can easily arrange that, too, if you go through a tour operator. **Chris Rowthorn Tours** (www.chrisrowthorn. com/geisha_tours), for example, can arrange a *kaiseki* dinner in the company of an interpreter and *geisha* for ¥70,000 (per group), plus the additional dinner cost (about ¥15,000 to ¥20,000) per person.

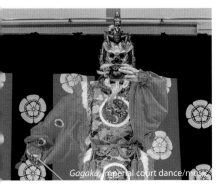

Gagaku, imperial court dance/music

Kanze Kaikan

The **Kanze Kaikan** noh theater in Okazaki, is a major venue for *noh* (a classical and slow-moving musical drama) and *kyogen* (a traditional form of comic theater), with about a dozen performances on its beautiful wooden stage each month. For non-Japanese speakers, both *noh* and *kyogen* can be hard to digest, but for a deeper look into these classical performance arts than offered at Gion Corner (page 66), and a glimpse at an array of Japanese traditions and formalities, Kanze Kaikan is the place. *Ten minutes from Higashiyama Station on the Tozai Line. The website, www.kyoto-kanze.jp, has the schedule for the year and details of fees (which vary), but is in Japanese only.*

Minami-za

The beautifully restored **Minami-za** kabuki theater on Shijo-dori is more than just an endearing landmark—as the oldest *kabuki* venue in Japan, dating to 1610, it also attracts the biggest performers in the field. Like many other traditional forms of theater, *kabuki* isn't easily accessible to first-timers, but no matter how much one fails to grasp the highly stylized dance-drama, it is nevertheless stunning on the eyes and you can get audio guidance in English

to help understand what's going on. You can also get tickets for single acts, which is a lot easier for a first visit than trying to sit through the typical several hours plus. *A one-minute walk from Kawaramachi Station on the Hankyu Line or Shijo-Kawaramachi bus station. www.kabuki-bito.jp/eng. Ticket prices vary, but start from around ¥4,000.*

BARS, PUBS & CLUBS

Craft Beer at Bungalow

Over the last decade or so Japan has undergone a craft beer revolution. Where once mass-produced brands like Asahi and Kirin were the only option, a loosening of regulation has seen an army of smaller brewers (not to mention established *sake* breweries) arrive on the beer scene, and so too craft beer pubs have sprung up from Hokkaido to Okinawa. You can even find the occasional craft beer in supermarkets nowadays; something unimaginable a decade ago. Kyoto might not be as crafty as Tokyo yet, but with bars like **Bungalow** you can get a laid-back taste of some of Japan's best craft beers—look for domestic craft pioneers like Baird and Shiga Kogen, amongst others, on the 10 taps. They also serve bar food and organic wines. *A couple of hundred meters east along Shijo-dori from Shijo-Omiya Station. Open 5 p.m.–2 a.m. Closed Tuesday. www.bungalow.jp.*

Drinks and Art at Tranq Room

Part bar, part café, part contemporary gallery, part intimate live music venue, **Tranq Room** on Shirakawa-dori (on bus routes 5, 93, 203 and 204) is a chill out favorite with Kyoto's artier residents; a great venue for a laidback drink and with a pretty good bet that something creative will be going on while you are there.

Many casual eateries spill out into the street

They also serve a decent curry, cakes and some organic fare. For something in a similar vein, also check out **A-Womb** (www.awomb.com). *Tranq Room is open noon to midnight. Closed Tuesdays. http://home.att.ne.jp/sun/tranqroom.*

Try an Izakaya

There are *izakaya* everywhere in Japan, from popular budget chains to simple neighborhood haunts to refined dining spots. What these watering hole-cum-restaurants have in common is a range of dishes and drinks, from beer and *sake* to *sashimi* (raw fish slices), *yakitori* (char-grilled chicken) and beyond. They are the perfect places for sampling an array of local flavors. Chains, such as **Shirokiya** and **Wara Wara** (both owned by the same company), have benefits such as picture menus and sometimes English explanations of the food. For extra quality, however, try somewhere like the natural-wood surrounds of **Uroco**, which specializes in charcoal-grilled meats and vegetables, alongside offering other usual *izakaya* dishes. To make things easy, consider opting for a course and seeing what comes; and maybe try washing it down with one of the dozen or so brands of *sake* on the menu, or something like a *shochu* (a spirit made from rice, potato or barley). If you can't get in, there'll always be something like a Wara Wara nearby. *Uroco is one minute from Kawaramachi Station. Courses from ¥3,000. Open daily 5 p.m.–2 a.m. www.uroco-kyoto.com. There's a Wara Wara just north of Kyoto Station (next to Kyoto Tower) but you can find lots more of them and Shirokiya in Kyoto and Nara via the shop search, in English, at www.monteroza.co.jp.*

Izakaya are great places to sample a variety of local flavors

Yoramu *Sake* Bar

Sake, usually referred to as *Nihonshu*, is the quintessential Japanese drink, and there is no shortage of places to try it in Kyoto or Nara. **Yoramu** finds its way onto this page as the *sake* representative for a couple of good reasons. First, it's hard to know what you are drinking, if you don't speak Japanese, but Yoramu's owner is an English-speaker from the Middle East who is more than happy to share his *Nihonshu* passion with newbies. Second, if you are going to try *sake*, try something good, instead of being put off trying it again by something bland—Yoramu has a great selection of *sake* that's full of character. Third, food. The Japanese don't tend to drink on an empty stomach, and Yoramu has Kyoto and Middle Eastern dishes that match the *sake* perfectly. Consider starting with the three *sake* taster set and go from there. ***Open 6 p.m.–midnight (during the day it is a soba noodle restaurant). Wednesday to Saturday. www. sakebar-yoramu.com.***

Japan's most recognizable tipple: *sake*

Live Music at Taku Taku or Greenwich House

In business since 1975, and housed in what was once a *sake* brewery, **Taku Taku** hosts mostly local rock, indie, punk, and blues acts, but occasionally has a well-known overseas performer or band on the bill. Whatever is on, given Taku Taku's reputation as one of the city's best venues, it'll likely draw a decent crowd. And whatever is on, it's a good place to have a few drinks and experience a very typical night in a Japanese "livehouse". Taku Taku is tough to find, but there is a map on the Japanese language-only website: www.geisya. or.jp/~takutaku. The simplest directions: come out of exit 11 of Kawaramachi Station (on the Hankyu Line). From there

it's two and bit blocks south of Shijo-dori. Tickets for many gigs can be bought at the door. If that isn't your scene, then nearby you could try the small café-cum-bar (it'll barely fit 20, including a band) **Greenwich House** (www.greenwich-house.com) for live jazz. It's a couple of blocks north of Shijo-dori and you can just pop in without tickets.

Clubbing at Lab Tribe and Metro

Kyoto has a lively and varied club scene. For techno and house, **Lab Tribe** (labtribe.net), one minute from exit 16 of Kyoto Shiyakusho-mae Station, is a fairly no frills, but extremely popular venue that also boast a great sound system. More eclectic and arguably Kyoto's most famous club, the welcoming **Metro** (www.metro.ne.jp; one minute from Jingu Marutamachi Station) puts on disco nights, Britpop nights, funk nights, and almost anything else beyond and between. They also have a promotion to attract foreigners—show your ID and get one free drink.

BEST SHOPPING

From fine kimono to bargain antiques—Kyoto is a shopper's paradise

When it comes to shopping in Kyoto, with numerous shopping districts and traditional stores there are plenty places to find the perfect souvenir or mementos. Just stroll along **Nishiki-koji food market** (page 34), the **Teramachi arcade** (page 34) or **Kawaramachi Street** (page 35), and you won't need to search hard to find something special to take home with you. Look in Chapter 2 and we have also highlighted some great shopping spots within each of the guided days out. If you are after something specific—be that pottery, fabrics or antiques—here are some of the best places to head for.

Chirimen Fabrics at Manekinekonote
Located within Nishiki-koji food market,

which is generally known for food, this store specializes in sometimes cute, sometimes inventive uses for traditional, high-quality *chirimen* fabric, with products such as colorful fabric-covered wallets and purses, key rings, aprons, business card holders, and many other items—things that have a very Japanese look plus an everyday function, and that don't hurt the wallet as a souvenir in the way that antiques or the finest *kimono* would. *Open daily 10 a.m.–6 p.m. www.manekinekonote.jp.*

Nishiki-koji food market is Kyoto's oldest food market

The flea market at To-ji Temple

Flea Market at To-ji temple

In all parts of Japan, temple grounds often seem to turn themselves over to flea markets. Kyoto's temples are no exception, and none is better than the flea market that appears at To-ji temple on the 21st of every month. With somewhere in the region of 1,000 vendors, there's a wide, wide range of items to search through here, from antiques, ceramics and *kimono* to tools, bric-a-brac and food. If you aren't in town on the 21st, then there is usually a smaller market here on the first Sunday of the month that's also worth checking out. *Held every 21st from early morning until around 4 p.m. To-ji is a 15-minute walk to the southwest of JR Kyoto Station, or a five-minute walk from To-ji Station on the Kintetsu Kyoto Line.*

Kimono and Fabrics at Mimuro

As with many traditional Japanese items, there are plenty of places in Kyoto and Nara to buy a *kimono*. For ease of access, range of selection and helpfulness, Mimuro ranks among the best. The five floors here have somewhere in the region of 50,000 items in all, including *kimono* across a range of price levels and all the essential accessories to go with them, such as *obi* (the sash that goes around the waist when wearing a *kimono*). They also have 1,500 colorful, cotton *yukata* gowns in stock, as well as *jinbei* (which look a bit like pajamas) for men—both common sights among the crowds at summer festivals. *Open daily 10 a.m.–6.30 p.m. A five-minute walk from Shijo Station or Hankyu Karasuma Station. Map at www.mimuro.net.*

Kiyomizu Pottery at Asahido

Located, along with many other ceramic stores, near Kiyomizu Temple (page 11), Asahido has been specializing in the local Kiyomizuyaki ceramics since 1870; a style defined by its enamel overglaze and Chinese-influenced decorations. The finest Kiyomizuyaki doesn't come cheaply, but further down the street (walking away from the temple) Asahido also has a general craft shop called Asahido Touan with items such as ceramics and textiles made by younger artisans at much lower prices. *Near the gates to Kiyomizu Temple, which is accessed via the Gojozaka bus stop by City Bus #206 from Kyoto Station. Open 9 a.m.–6 p.m. daily. www.asahido.co.jp.*

Kiyomizu pottery

Kyoto Handicraft Center

thing for everyone. *Open daily 10 a.m.-7 p.m. www.kyotohandicraftcenter.com.*

Japanese Teas at Fukujuen

The six floors of tea trader Fukujuen's flagship store on Shijo-dori (page 35) are a green tea lover's paradise. From tea utensils and bowls for sale, plus a variety of local high-grade teas from Uji (page 46), to opportunities to try the tea ceremony (see page 78 for other places) and learn about Japanese tea and the correct way to prepare and serve it, Fukujuen has pretty much everything covered. They also have a nice café where visitors can try tea along with traditional sweets, as well as a restaurant where French cuisine gets a Japanese twist with green tea heavy on the menu. *Open 11 a.m.-7 p.m. Closed third Wednesday of the month. Ten minutes east of Shijo Station on Shijo-dori. Map at www.fukujuen-kyotohonten.com.*

Kyoto Handicraft Center

Across the road from the north-west corner of Heian Jingu (page 38), with English-speaking staff on all floors and able to take a dozen currencies, Kyoto Handicraft Center is the most tourist-friendly place to pick up a traditional souvenir, whether it's a woodblock print, ceramics, *Nambu* ironware, lacquerware, or all manner of other fine work. The center also sells *kimono* and *yukata* robes, as well as simple t-shirts and other typical souvenirs. There's pretty much some-

SHOPPING FOR ANTIQUES

Not surprisingly for such a historic city, Kyoto is known for the number and qual-

The streets near Kiyomizu Temple are full of interesting shops

ity of its antique stores, many of which are concentrated in two main areas: the covered **Teramachi arcade**, which is featured as part of the day out in Central Kyoto on page 33, and the Ohto area (in particular **Shinmonzen-dori**) north of Gion (page 30) on the eastern side of the Kamogawa River. Just pottering about these two areas, you'll come across all sorts, from old ceramics and scrolls to tea ceremony paraphernalia and Buddhist items. If you want to find something particular, the Ohto Antiques Association's website (www.kobijutsu-kyoto. jp/english) is a great place to start, as it lists all several dozen antique, art and craft stores in and around Shinmonzen-dori. Sadly, the official Teramachi shop association guide, which is equally good, is only in Japanese: www.kyo-teramachi. com. If you don't fancy going online, here is a selection of the best picks for antiques in the two areas:

Renkodo Located on Shinmonzen-dori, the specialty here is exquisite Imari blue-and-white porcelain from the Edo era. Open 11 a.m.–6 p.m. daily.
Nanmeido Just east of Renkodo on Shinmonzen-dori, Nanmeido has a variety of Asian antiques, including tea sets, calligraphy items, and Buddhist art. Open 9 a.m.–6 p.m., with irregular days off.
Konjaku Nishimura A short walk from Shinmonzen-dori, Nishimura has a colorful collection of antique clothing such as *kimono* and *obi*, as well as other valuable old textiles. www.konjaku.com. Open 10 a.m.–7 p.m., closed Wednesdays.
Kyoto Antiques Center On the northern, uncovered end of Teramachi-dori, here you'll find a broad selection of both Asian and Western antiques, including ceramics, dolls, and jewelry. Open 10.30 a.m.–7 p.m., closed third Tuesday of the month. www.antique-shinagawa.com.

SHOPPING IN NARA

Mochiidono Center Gai
South of Kintetsu Nara Station, following on from the covered Higashimuki mall, this shopping street has an eclectic mix of stores, from used books to crafts and hipster fashions to standard souvenir and sweet shops. It's all a far cry from the street's roots, which apparently date back over 1,000 years as a market area.

The Nara-machi Area
A cobweb of alleys lined with old wooden buildings, many of which are registered as cultural heritage properties, the Nara-machi area (see page 48 for more as part of a day out in Nara) a kilometer or so south of Kintetsu Nara Station and most easily reached by Mochiidono Center Gai, is home to a number of stores selling local ceramics and handmade trinkets, not to mention tea dealers, galleries, and artisans. Like the Mochiidono Center Gai, it's a good place to potter; good for finding something beyond the run-of-the-mill souvenir stores you'll find selling key rings, fans and the like near the main attractions. One particular Nara-machi store to look out for is Kai (www.kai.st), which houses half a dozen craft shops under one roof.

Useful shopping phrases
How much is (this)? *(kore) wa ikura desu ka?*
Do you accept credit cards? *Kurejitto kaado wa tsukaemasu ka?*
It's too expensive: *Taka sugimasu*
I'll take this: *Kore o kudasai*
Do you have…? *…wa arimasu ka?*
Cash: *Genkin*

KID-FRIENDLY ATTRACTIONS

For when the kids have seen one temple too many . . .

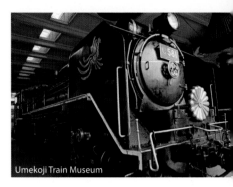
Umekoji Train Museum

Temple hopping, tea ceremonies and *kaiseki-ryori* can be unforgettable experiences for adults, but nigh on unbearable for kids. For smaller children who just need somewhere to run around and burn energy, places like Kyoto Imperial Palace Park (page 33) and Maruyama Park (page 28) can provide a few fun hours, as can Nara Park (page 48), where the kids could feed "deer crackers" to the mostly laid-back deer that live in the park. You could even head to the Kamogawa River (page 35) in Kyoto for a paddle. Better yet, schedule in visits to some of the kid-friendly attractions below.

Umekoji Train Museum

This might bore some kids, but it's the perfect place for train buffs, be they what the Japanese call *tetsudou otaku* (geeks into photographing trains), *kotetsu* (train-obsessed kids) and *mamatetsu* or *papatetsu* (the mums and dads that follow their kids into train obsession). This museum has 19 steam engines on display from the Meiji, Taisho and Showa eras as well as other train-related exhibits that are housed in a former station building. Three times a day, you can also take a 10-minute ride on one of the steam engines (from 11 a.m., 1.30 p.m. and 3.30 p.m.). It's a 20-minute walk west from Kyoto Station or you can take a city bus from the bus terminal at Kyoto Station to the Umekoji-koen-mae bus stop. *Open 9.30 a.m.–4.30 p.m. Closed Mondays. Admission ¥200 (children ¥100). See: http://www.mtm.or.jp/uslm.*

Kyoto Aquarium

Billing itself as a place for "Edutainment", Kyoto Aquarium has nine well-designed zones that give an enjoyable and insightful look at a wide range of aquatic life. These include a zone on sea animals, which is home to seals, a zone on Kyoto's rivers, one on penguins, a dolphin lagoon that puts on dolphin shows (I know, not the best way for a dolphin to spend its days, but it's a step up from being culled in Taiji), as well as a 500-ton ocean pool that offers a panoramic ocean scene. From Kyoto Station, it's an eight-minute ride on a City Bus #33, #205, #206 or #208 to the Kyoto Aquarium bus stop. You can also easily combine it with the Umekoji Train Museum, which is on the other side of the same park. *Open daily 8 a.m.–5 p.m. Adults ¥2,050, with several lower rates for children and teens. www. kyoto-aquarium.com.*

Kyoto International Manga Museum

Housed in a former elementary school, the KIMM is home to some 300,000 comics (*manga*) and related exhibits, almost all of which you are allowed to pick up and read, whether propped up against the wall, cross-legged on the floor in one of the hallways, or flat out on the old school lawn. The Japanese are never shy about reading anywhere (just visit a convenience store, where people will spend ages having a free read), but this takes that to new levels. While the majority of the comics are in Japanese, the imagery in them means many transcend language barriers, and there are also a fair number in English and other languages. It's also worth checking the schedule before coming to try and time your visit with a live drawing demonstration. You'll find the museum one minute on foot from exit 2 of Karasuma Oike Station on the Karasuma and Tozai subway lines. Buses #15, #51, #61, #62, and #63 also stop nearby at the Karasuma Oike bus stop. *Open 10 a.m.–6 p.m. (last entry 5.30pm). Closed Wednesdays. Adults ¥800, kids ¥300. See: www.kyotomm.jp.*

TOEI Studio Park

Also known just as Eigamura, this super-kitsch theme park-slash-TV and movie set is designed to look like an Edo-era town and allows visitors to wander around in period costumes while taking in exhibits on the host of TV shows and movies made here. Besides that, you can also delve into the tricks and traps of a ninja house and other mock buildings and (this is the best bit) watch live samurai battles and ninja shows that are brilliantly over the top. It's near JR Uzamasa Station and served directly by Kyoto buses #61 to #65 and City Bus #75. *Open daily at least 9.30 a.m.–4.30 p.m. (check the website for specific days). Adults ¥2,200, kids half that. See: www.toei-eigamura.com.*

Universal Studios in Osaka

Opened in 2001, USJ has given the Kansai region something to rival the magical allure of Tokyo's Disneyland, even though the 8 million visitors each year to USJ is barely half the number who enter the Magic Kingdom. I'd happily let Kansai have Disney in return for having USJ on my doorstep in Tokyo, and with it easy access to USJ's cool simulators, white-knuckle rides and kid-friendly attractions based on movies like Shrek and Spiderman (both of which feature in mind-blowing 4D rides). Other movies with their own attractions here include Jaws, Back to the Future, and Jurassic Park, while there are also cuter attractions featuring Hello Kitty and Sesame Street characters.

To get there, from Kyoto Station take the JR Kyoto Line to Osaka Station (30 mins), then change to the JR Osaka Loop Line and head to Nishi-kujo Station (5 mins). From there, the same train becomes the Yumesaki Line, which can be a bit confusing. Stay on board for another five minutes to Universal City Station, which serves the theme park. All told, it'll take an hour and cost just over ¥1,000. *Open daily from at least 9.30 a.m.–8 p.m. A one-day pass for the park costs ¥6,980 for adults and ¥4,880 for under-12s. See: www.usj.co.jp/e.*

The Aoi Matsuri

FESTIVALS & EVENTS

All year round, Kyoto and Nara host many colorful *matsuri*

Be it annual celebrations of the seasons or re-enactments of ancient processions, the people of Kyoto and Nara, like the rest of Japan, love a good *matsuri* (festival). Before you go, take a look at the extensive list of events (broken down by month) at www.KyotoGuide.com and you will find a traditional event of some form or other— big or small—to check out during your trip. With any luck, your time in Kyoto and Nara might even coincide with one of the five standout annual events below.

SPRING

Cherry Blossom Viewing

Cherry blossom season in any part of Japan is special, but there's something about Kyoto and Nara's traditional back-drops that enhances the blossom's allure. The wave of *sakura* that sweeps north-ward over Japan from mid-March to early May, usually casts its delicate pink spell on the two cities for a couple of weeks in mid- to late March or early April (it varies slightly every year). The Okazaki Canal near Heian Jingu (page 38) in Kyoto ex-plodes with color through which tour boats gently cruise. Bathed in pink, Maruyama Park behind Yasaka Shrine (page 28) attracts crowds of picnickers. Arashiyama (page 40) and the Philosopher's Path (page 36) are two more of many locations that are given a fabulous pink makeover. In Nara, it has to be Nara Park (page 48), which sees 1,700 *sakura* trees in bloom, for a brief moment drawing the attention of visitors away from the park's marauding deer.

Aoi Matsuri

Dating back some 1,400 years to the reign of the Emperor Kinmei, the Aoi Matsuri apparently came about in reac-tion to a poor grain harvest. At the time considered to be the result of an angry god, rites were performed to remove his curse and a bumper harvest soon fol-lowed. The rites soon became an annual fixture and have since morphed into the current Aoi Matsuri, which is held on May 15. The *matsuri's* main event sees a procession (starting at 10.30 a.m. from Kyoto Imperial Palace) of two oxcarts, four cows, 36 horses, and 600 people dressed in traditional Heian-era clothing and all decorated with lush green *aoi* leaves, gently parade to Shimogamo Shrine and finally Kamigamo Shrine, where shrine rites are performed. As an entertaining aside, other events also take place, most notably a demonstration of horseback archery (*yabusame*) after the procession.

SUMMER

Gion Matsuri

While many festivals are rooted in cel-ebration—welcoming spring, commemo-rating historical events, and the like—Kyoto's biggest festival comes from far less auspicious beginnings. The Gion Matsuri began as a rite to ward off a plague that hit Kyoto in the 860s. More than 1,000 years on, the modern-day festival now spans the full month of July, although with its main events happen-ing from July 14–17. The highlight comes on the 17th, when 32 elaborately deco-rated floats carrying musicians and dancers dressed in traditional clothing parade through central Kyoto. At the same time, many areas become pedestri-anized, allowing food and festival stalls to set up to feed and entertain hundreds of thousands of festival-goers who de-scend upon the city.

Daimon-ji Gozan Fire Festival

The Daimon-ji Gozan Fire Festival (Daimon-ji Gozan Okuribi) is one of those events you'll definitely want your camera for (and want your camera to have a good night setting for). On August 16, as the culmination of the annual O-bon celebra-tions (during which the spirits of ances-tors are honored), five giant mountainside

Kyoto's Gion Matsuri

fires are lit around Kyoto, each a *kanji* character. Visible from all over the city, it starts with the character for "large" (*dai*; 大), measuring about 80 by 120 meters (265 x 395 feet), at 8 p.m., with the other fires being lit at 10-minute intervals thereafter to give the spirits a warm send off as the return to their graves for an-other year. The banks of the Kamogawa River are a good spot for taking in the views. See www.kyokanko.or.jp/okuribi.

AUTUMN

Jidai Matsuri

Begun in 1895 to celebrate the 1,100th anniversary of Kyoto becoming the Imperial capital (even though Kyoto was no longer the capital by this time), this festival emanating from Heian Jingu (page 38) on October 22 is defined by an afternoon procession of 2,000 people in historic attire (dressed as everything from samurai to commoners) through central Kyoto, along with a procession of portable shrines (*mikoshi*) accompanied by traditional court music. The event offers a magical glimpse of ancient Japan.

BEST CULTURAL EXPERIENCES

Go deeper into traditional Japan

Traditional Japan can feel impenetrable at times, but it is possible to go under its surface in places with just a little effort. In historic cities like Kyoto and Nara, in particular, your visit will be even more memorable if you take the time to experience a slice of "old Japan" like the tea ceremony, soak in hot spring bath or pause for Zen meditation.

Try the Tea Ceremony

The tea ceremony has long held an important position in traditional Japanese culture. Known mostly as *chado* or *sado* in Japanese and with numerous slight variations depending on the particular tea ceremony "school", the Zen-influenced ritual is performed with both calm precision and grace, turning the otherwise

simple process of mixing powdered green tea (*matcha*) and hot water into one of Japan's finer forms of artistic expression. Nowhere is more fitting a place to try it yourself than in Kyoto.

To learn about the specific turns of the cup, how and when to sip, how to hold the cup, when to bow and when not, and the many other intricacies of the ceremony, there are quite a few good places that now offer classes or one-off experiences in English. The tourist information center (page 92) has details on many of these, but a few especially worth mentioning here are En, Ju-An, and Ran Hotei: **En**, in Gion (www.teaceremonyen.com), does four short ceremonies daily in English for ¥2,000 per person; **Ran Hotei** (www.ranhotei.com), a teahouse and café set in a renovated old townhouse, offers a 90-minute tea ceremony lesson with Canadian tea master Randy for ¥2,500; and **Ju-An** (www.teaceremonykyoto.com), near Kyoto Station, provides a two-part tea ceremony workshop at ¥2,000 per person.

Zen Meditation

Zazen ("seated meditation") is a core component of Zen practice, and although certain different schools of Buddhism take slightly different approaches to meditating—to get into a meditative state, for example, some stress a focus on introspection, some use concentration, others try "non-thinking"—the eventual aim goal is essentially one: nothing; to let the world go by without interacting with it; to give up judgement; to let thoughts glide by like clouds. Even if you aren't on a mission to "find yourself", from both a cultural perspective and in terms of just being very relaxing, experiencing *zazen* is extremely worthwhile. In Kyoto, quite a few places offer *zazen* in Japanese, but **Shunkoin Temple** (page

Sushi cooking class

58), offers excellent, almost daily meditation sessions from 8.30 a.m. in English for just ¥1,000 under the guidance of the bilingual Rev. Kawakami. It's best to check the schedule (shunkoinzentemple. blogspot.jp) before turning up, but usually no reservations are required.

Cooking Classes and Tours

Food is such an integral part of Japanese culture and of any trip to Kyoto and Nara, it should come as no surprise that there are dozens upon dozens of culinary schools and teach-from-home instructors offering cooking classes in English for international travelers. Here are some of the many that are worth a look: **Cooking Sun** (www.cooking-sun. com), in Shimogyo Ward, has 3.5-hour lessons with Japanese teachers in which you'll learn to cook five to six traditional dishes (things like rolled *sushi*, *tempura*, bean jellies and so on) at a cost of ¥5,000 to ¥7,800 per person; **Roujiya** (kyotobase.com/cooking), just south of Nijo Castle, has 3-hour lessons for groups of two to four (¥5,000 per person) where you'll make and eat *sushi*, side dishes, soup, and dessert, and also learn about Japanese table manners and etiquette; or there's **Viator's** (www. viator.com) **Kyoto Cooking Class**, *Sake* **Tasting** and **Nishiki Tour** (book online;

$100 per person), which gets great reviews and includes a 90-minute cooking lesson (rolled *sushi*), visit to a *sake* museum and a two-hour guided tour around the sights and scents of the wonderful Nishiki-koji food market (page 34).

Other Cultural Classes

From pottery to tie-dyeing, Kyoto and Nara have all manner of hands-on, one-off classes on offer. As well as the cultural activities already listed in this section, another of the more popular is *ikebana* flower arranging, which you could try at **Kafu** (kafu.co) close to Higashiyama Station with a 90-minute class for ¥5,000 per person. Kafu also runs cooking, calligraphy, *sake* and tea ceremony classes, among other things. Another fun craft to try is *origami*, and you can do sessions for ¥3,800 per person through **WAK** (wakjapan.com; a few blocks south of Kyoto Imperial Palace), who also have *kimono* wearing workshops, other craft classes, and so on. A good resource for finding other possibilities is the Kyoto Prefecture's Welcome to Kyoto website, which lists 50 or so workshops, small museums and other places that offer cultural classes: www.pref.kyoto.jp/visitkyoto/en/theme/ activities/cultural/crafts.

Making *origami*

BEST GALLERIES & MUSEUMS

History, contemporary art and artisanal crafts

For artifacts, art and artisanal work, Kyoto and Nara deliver everything from prestigious museums to craft centers and hip contemporary galleries. The Nishijin Textile Center (page 24) and the Kyoto International Manga Museum (page 33) are both covered already in Chapter 2. Here are a handful of other places to delve into Japanese creativity both ancient and modern.

Kyoto National Museum

Opened in 1897, the redbrick building of Kyoto National Museum houses Kyoto's finest collection of Japanese artifacts, with three floors of exhibition space that covers metalwork, textiles and costumes, Buddhist paintings, calligraphy, illustrated handscrolls, archaeological relics, and more. The collection also spreads outdoors, with sculptures from the Korean peninsula dotting the museum's East Garden and early stone Buddhas and foundation stones among the things accenting the West Garden. To add a European touch, there's also a cast of Rodin's "The Thinker" on the grounds. *Open Tuesday to Sunday 9.30 a.m.–5 p.m. Admission ¥520. From Kyoto Station take City Bus #206 or #208 to Hakubutsukan Sanjusangendo-mae. Or a seven-minute walk from Shichijo Station. www.kyohaku. go.jp.*

Kyoto Museum of Traditional Crafts

Otherwise known as the Fureaikan,

there are 77 different kinds of crafts on display (and many of these are for sale) at this museum's permanent exhibition, complete with detailed info on their roots and how they are made. Along with that, there are regular thematic exhibitions that go deeper into specific crafts through artisan demonstrations and workshops, plus opportunities for visitors to try making their own crafts, such as Kyoto stencil-dyeing (*surigata-yuzen*). For anyone with even a passing interest in crafts, it's not to be missed. *Ten minutes from Higashiyama Station on the Tozai Line or take City Bus #5 or #100 to Kyoto-kaikan Bijutsukan-mae. Open daily 9 a.m.–5 p.m. Free. www.miya-komesse.jp/fureaika.*

Ii Museum

Specializing in armor and swords, the Ii Museum offers a fascinating look into feudal Japan and the world of shogun and samurai. To be honest, the cost of admission (¥1,500) might be a bit much if Japanese history and weaponry isn't your thing; but, if it is, then the collection put together by Mr. Tatsuo Ii (the museum's owner and an expert on historic armory) is excellent. On top of that, the museum also exhibits a collection of letters and scrolls that, while hard to decipher even for Japanese readers at times, are simply beautiful historical documents. *Admission ¥1,500. Open 1 p.m.–5 p.m. Closes irregularly, so it is best to call before visiting. Ten minutes from Gion-Shijo Station on the Keihan Line, map online: www.ii-museum.jp.*

Kyoto Garden of Fine Arts

Designed by legendary contemporary Japanese architect Tadao Ando, a Pritzker Prize winner who, self-taught, became an architect after being both an amateur boxer and a trucker, the open-air

Kyoto Garden of Fine Arts

(but sunk below ground level) Kyoto Garden of Fine Arts features Ando's distinctive usage of rough concrete and airy spaces, in which it houses copies of famous (and giant) works of art on ceramic tiles. Among the collection, there's a full-size version of Michelangelo's *Last Judgment*, the original of which is in the Sistine Chapel, that's been photo-engrave onto 110 ceramic tiles, as well as a version of Da Vinci's *Last Supper*. The classic art on ceramics is striking, but even more so in its ultra-sleek setting—and like everything Ando has designed, the museum is worth visiting for the architecture alone. *Open daily 9 a.m.–5 p.m. A one-minute walk from exit 3 of Kitayama Station on the Karasuma subway line (six stops north of Shijo and eight north of Kyoto). Admission ¥100. www.kyoto-toban-hp.or.jp.*

National Museum of Modern Art

Located near Heian Jingu (page 38), the MOMAK (to use its nickname) is a welcome counter-balance to Kyoto's ancient sights. A visit here might coincide with a bit of Warhol on display or some 1970s ceramics; or maybe a collection of Pointillism work or photography will take center stage. Either way, the collection of Japanese and overseas contemporary art here is always worth a look. *Open Tuesday to Sunday 9 a.m.–5 p.m. (until 8 p.m. on Fridays from April to mid-August). Closes for exhibition changeovers, so check before going. Take City Bus #5 or #100 from Kyoto Station to Okazaki Koen/Bijutsukan,Heian Jingu-mae. www. momak.go.jp.*

Nara National Museum

Housed in Western-style buildings that date to the 1880s, the Nara National Museum is certainly one of Nara Park's (page 48) most striking sights, as well as being home to one of the better collections of Japanese and other Asian art and artifacts in the country. The exhibits here include Buddhist sculptures, ancient calligraphy and religious paintings, plus archaeological finds dating back as far as the Jomon period (10th–4th century BC) and a collection of ancient Chinese bronzes. *Open Tuesday to Sunday 9.30 a.m.–5 p.m. (closes Tuesday, if the Monday before was a national holiday). In Nara Park (page 48). Admission ¥500. www.narahaku.go.jp.*

TRAVEL TIPS

From navigating the airport on arrival and finding your way around Kyoto's transport network to learning a few useful words of Japanese, this short A to Z guide covers all the essentials you will need (and some you hopefully won't) to make your time in Kyoto and Nara as hassle free as possible.

Arriving in Kyoto

Kyoto doesn't have its own international airport, but there are two airports close to Kyoto, so you don't necessarily have to fly to Tokyo. Here are the options:

ARRIVING FROM KANSAI AIPORT (KIX)

With more than 50 airlines serving the airport, KIX (www.kansai-airport.or.jp/en) is Japan's second international airport. The easiest **rail option** for traveling between KIX and Kyoto is the JR Haruka limited express train (¥3,490; 75 mins; first service from KIX at 6.33 a.m., last at 10.16 p.m.; in the other direction the first is 5.45 a.m., last 8.16 p.m.). You don't need to book tickets in advance. You could also take the **bus** without needing to book tickets. Osaka Air Transport (www.okk-bus.co.jp/en) has buses running from KIX from 6 a.m. to 11.40 p.m. and from Kyoto Station to KIX from 4.30 a.m.–9.10 p.m. Tickets are ¥2,550 each way or ¥4,180 return (with cheaper rates for kids) and the journey takes about one hour and 40 minutes. A final option, which can be good for groups, is to take a **Skygate Shuttle minibus** run by MK Taxi (www.mktaxi-japan.com). It delivers you right to your hotel door, costs ¥3,600 per person and requires advance booking on the website.

ARRIVING FROM OSAKA (ITAMI) AIRPORT

If you come through Itami (http://osaka-airport.co.jp/en), the best option is the **bus**. Osaka Air Transport has services running from Itami to Kyoto Station from 8 a.m. to 9.10 p.m. and from Kyoto Station to Itami from 5.50 a.m. to 6.55 p.m. Tickets are ¥1,310 each way (half that for kids) and the journey takes about 55 minutes. You can buy tickets on the day. As with KIX (above), MK Taxi also run a bookable **minibus service** to Kyoto that delivers you right to your hotel (www.mktaxi-japan.com; ¥2,400 per person).

FROM TOKYO OR NARITA BY TRAIN

If you are coming to Kyoto from Tokyo, the easiest way is to catch a **high-speed** *shinkansen* **(bullet train) from Tokyo or Shinagawa stations.** Tickets can be bought at the station and services run every 10 minutes or so. The fastest service is the direct Nozomi, which takes 2 hours and 17 minutes (¥13,910 one way), and there is also a slower, but also direct Hikari service (2 hours 49 minutes). A much cheaper (from ¥3,000), but much, much slower option is to **take a bus**. Willer Express is a good option for that: http://travel.willer.co.jp. **If you are coming to Kyoto straight from Narita Airport**, first take the Narita Express train (www.jreast.co.jp/e/nex; ¥3,020) to Tokyo Station, and get the *shinkansen* from there.

Major Events in Kyoto and Nara

Kyoto and Nara both have many wonderful annual events—some celebrated in other parts of Japan, some unique to the cities. The best of these, including the historic **Gion Matsuri** in Kyoto in July and the annual **cherry blossom viewing** in spring, are covered in Chapter Three (page 76). To find other events that might be on when you are visiting, check out the excellent month-by-month listings on the official **Kyoto Convention** and **Visitors Bureau** website (www.kyoto.travel/plan_your_visit/cultural_events) and the website of the **Nara City Sightseeing Information Center** (http://narashikanko.or.jp/en).

Climate and Seasons

Spring (*haru*) in Kyoto and Nara is glorious, hinted at initially with the plum blossom of late February and early March and then heralded by a pink front of cherry blossom in late March and early April that signals the arrival of pleasantly warm temperatures that last through May.

Separating spring from summer is a three-to four-week **rainy season** (*tsuyu*) straddling June and July, during which the heat and humidity start to rise and the skies are often grey. Given the heat and humidity, raincoats can be a bit too much to wear, so pick up a cheap umbrella instead (all convenience stores have them for less than $5) and dress lightly.

After rainy season, the rain gives way to clear **summer** (*natsu*) skies—occasionally punctuated by a typhoon—that last through to late September. Summer high temperatures are typically around 32°C (89°F) to 35°C (95°F) , and get close to touching 40°C (104°F) , with midnight lows around the 25°C (77°F) mark. Shorts/skirts and tee shirts or short-sleeved shirts will be fine everywhere, but you might want to bring one light set of smart clothes if you end up having *kaiseki-ryori*. A spare tee shirt in your bag, when you are out and about isn't a bad idea; you might be glad of a fresh change, especially if you end up inside in a damp top with the air conditioning set to freezing. Remember to take precautions against heatstroke—drink plenty of fluids, wear a hat and don't forget the sun block.

After several months of sweating and *natsu bate* (summer fatigue), the temperatures begin to drop with the start of **autumn** in October (and for a few weeks the likelihood of a typhoon hitting increases). Like spring, autumn is a fantastic time to visit Kyoto and Nara, as the skies tend to stay clear, the air feels fresh again, high temperatures hover in the low 20°Cs (70°Fs) and latterly high 10°Cs (50°Fs) and autumnal colors transform much of the cities and their most famous attractions.

Come December and the air starts to cool, with **winter** proper lasting through February. Kyoto and Nara tend to be quite dry and mild (and very often sunny), with

the temperature rarely dropping below 0°C (32°F) and often in excess of 10°C (50°F).

Electricity

The electrical current in western Japan, which includes Kyoto and Nara, is 100 volts, 60hz AC. If you also travel to eastern Japan, which includes Tokyo, it's 100 volts, 50hz alternating current (AC). Japanese sockets take plugs with two flat pins, so you may need to bring an adaptor.

Etiquette

Japanese society is guided by numerous subtle points of etiquette and social syntax; enough for row upon row of books to have been written about them, whether that be instructions on how to hand over a business card (give/receive with both hands, keep it on the table during the meeting, and don't scribble anything on it) or how to politely use chopsticks (I'm not the best person to ask about that, but don't point, gesture or skewer anything with them). Truth be told, however, as long as you follow simple universal manners, it would take something exceptional for a foreign visitor to upset the Japanese with a social faux pas—you simply aren't expected to know local manners. That said, there are a few local rules to bear in mind.
• Firstly, at a communal **bath** at a traditional inn (*ryokan*), public bathhouse (*sento*) or hot spring (*onsen*), don't get into the bath dirty or soapy. Use the separate wash area near the baths to shower and then rinse well before getting into the communal bathtub, making sure to get in fully naked and not let your wash cloth enter the water.
• Secondly, shoes. Remove your outdoor **footwear** and change into slippers (which will be prepared for you) whenever you enter a *ryokan* guestroom or someone's house. The same rule applies at many

temples, shrines and even certain restaurants and *izakaya*. The best way to judge when shoes aren't allowed is to look out for slippers at the entrance—if there are slippers lined up, use them, then leave your shoes by the entrance or, if available, store them in a footlocker. Once inside, remove your slippers before setting foot on any *tatami* mat flooring.

• Next, when **eating**, don't stand **chopsticks** in a bowl of rice or pass anything from chopstick to chopstick. Both have associations with death and funeral services. To be extra polite when eating, say *itadakimasu* (lit. I humbly receive) before starting and *gochisosama deshita* (lit. you were a feast) when finishing (or to staff when leaving a restaurant). Finally, and this will be good news for cheapskates, **tipping** is not done in Japan. Trying to tip somebody might even cause embarrassment or offense, so you have a ready-made excuse not to even thinking about doing it. For more about etiquette, visit the **Japan National Tourism Organization**'s website: www.jnto.or.jp.

Travelers with Disabilities

For travelers with disabilities Japan can be quite a challenge. Only a third of the country's train stations are fully accessible and many other public places lack basic facilities such as wheelchair ramps. Although major urban hotels tend to have wheelchair-friendly rooms and accessible public areas, *ryokan* and smaller hotels are often lacking such facilities. Looking specifically at Kyoto and Nara, many of the old narrow side streets really don't lend themselves to accessibility.

To look at the positives, newer public buildings and department stores or malls will have barrier-free toilets, access ramps and wide elevators. Many taxi companies also now have cars with chair lifts, even though these typically require

booking at least an hour in advance (in Kyoto, try MK Taxi; www.mktaxi-japan.com; 075-778-4141).

On the trains and subway at least one carriage will be designated for wheelchair users. Station staff can direct you to this and can also be called upon to help wheelchair users get on and off the train, using a fold-up ramp they keep in the station office to negotiate the gap between train and platform. Some stations also have chair lifts to get to and from the platforms, when elevators aren't available.

A handy resource is the **map of Kyoto designed for the elderly and those with disabilities**, which is available for free at the **Tourist Information Center at Kyoto Station** (page 92). For a much more in-depth guide to accessible attractions, restaurants, hotels, stations and more in Kyoto and Nara, also check out the excellent **Japan Accessible Tourism** Center: www.japan-accessible.com/tips.htm.

Getting around Kyoto

Kyoto is a fairly easy city to navigate, as the streets are arranged in an East-West/North-South grid pattern. If you have the time and energy, walking or cycling are by far the best ways to get around. Buses and taxis are also convenient to get from one area of the city to another.

BUSES

Almost all of Kyoto's main sights are covered by the city's extensive bus network, which is great value for money and easy to navigate. Before you start exploring pick up a ¥500 day-pass for the buses and an English-language copy of the Kyoto bus network map from either the Tourist Information Center in Kyoto Station (page 92) or the ticket office at the bus terminal on Kyoto Station's north side.

In most cases, you get on the bus at the

back and alight at the front, paying the driver (or showing your pass) as you get off. If you aren't using a day pass, fares within the city are a flat ¥220 per journey for adults and ¥110 for children (aged 6 to 12). Buses that leave the city center will cost more, depending on the destination. Most buses operate from about 6 a.m. through to 7 p.m., although some run later.

SUBWAY

Kyoto has **two subway lines**: the Karasuma subway line (running south-north and passing through Kyoto and Shijo stations) and Tozai subway line (east-west through the city center). Adult fares start from ¥210, children from ¥110. If you don't know how much your fare will be, just buy the cheapest ticket (from the vending machines near the ticket gate) and then adjust when you get to your destination (there will be a machine for doing that inside the tickets or, if not, you can pay at the counter by the gates).

If you are going to be out and about on the subway and buses all day, consider a **Kyoto Sightseeing One-day** (adult ¥1,200/children ¥600) or **Two-day Pass** (adult ¥2,000/children ¥1,000). For their duration they give unlimited access to city center buses and both subway lines.

TRAINS

The trains in Kyoto aren't quite as useful as the subway, because they don't serve most of the major attractions in the city. You may need them, however, when heading on excursions out of central Kyoto. As well as multiple JR (Japan Railways) Lines, you'll also find the Keihan Line (running from Sanjo-dori in Kyoto to Yodoyabashi in Osaka), the Hankyu Kyoto Line (running between the downtown Kawaramachi in Kyoto and Umeda in Osaka, and the Kintetsu network (reaching from Kyoto to in and around Nara, Osaka and other

areas in the region). One other line you might well use if you explore western Kyoto is the Randen Arashiyama Line, a tram that runs 7.2km from Shijo Omiya in central Kyoto to Arashiyama (page 40) in the west, and which has a shorter line branching north from its center (the Keifuku Kitano Line) that heads to Ryoan-ji (page 22) and Myoshin-ji (home to Shunkoin, page 58).

RENTING A BICYCLE

Bicycles are a great way to get around Kyoto and there are plenty of places that do affordable rentals by the day (some overnight, too) or in hour- to several-hour packages. Expect to pay from ¥200/hour and ¥1,000-plus/day. For a full guide of rental shops listed by area, check out the excellent www.cyclekyoto.com, which also has information on cycling routes around many of the areas covered in this book. They also list areas to avoid by bike (including Gion and Kiyomizu Temple). Before you cycle, make sure you read **Cycle Kyoto's guide to bicycle laws** and where to and not park, as this can save you a lot of money in fines and a lot of hassle from police looking to fill their bike crime quotas.

TAXIS

Taxis can be hailed down all over central Kyoto and will often be waiting near the major attractions and stations. Fares start at a minimum ¥630, which covers the first two kilometers (one and a quarter miles), and then rise the further you go. If you need to call a taxi, or if you want to arrange a driver for the day and guided tours, the following two taxi companies can handle English-speaking calls. **MK Taxi** (075-778-4141; www.mktaxi-japan.com): Regular taxi service and charters. **Yasaka Limousine & Taxi Service Corp**

Rickshaw Rides

Yes, it's very touristy, and no, you wouldn't see a local in a rickshaw, but don't discount the idea of a rickshaw ride. If you are unable to do much walking or if you feel like doing something a little kitsch, a rickshaw with an English-speaking driver/guide is a fun way to see certain parts of Kyoto. Typically, rickshaws are two-seaters

(and you can perch a small child on your lap, too) and companies tend to offer packages that run from a single block tour (about ten minutes) to two-hour tour, mostly on set routes (although they can customize). You'll find prices are fairly uniform between companies at about ¥8,000 (two people) for 30 minutes and ¥30,000 for two hours (two people), and you'll easily find rickshaws in places like Arashiyama, Ginkaku-ji, Kinkaku-ji and Gion without having to book. That said, choosing a course and booking in advance is never a bad idea, in which case a company like **Ebisuya** (http://ebisuya.com/en) is a good, English-speaking option, with routes that include a two-hour trip from Ginkaku-ji to Kiyomizu Temple and a variety of routes around Arashiyama.

(075-842-1214; www.yasaka.jp/english): English-speaking driver-guides, tailor-made itineraries and experiential tours.

Health and Safety

Like the rest of Japan, Kyoto and Nara are by and large safe places to visit. Health wise, the cities have an advanced medical services infrastructure, and, if necessary, you will be able to locate clinics and hospitals that can treat you in English (see page 92 for emergency contact information). Additionally, Japan doesn't have any requirements for pre-travel inoculation against known diseases, drinking water is safe and you won't need to worry about major water-borne or insect-borne diseases (although in 2014 Tokyo had its first outbreak of Dengue Fever in 70 years). That said, there are certain precautions to keep in mind when planning and during your visit.

While over-the-counter **drugs and medications** are widely available at pharmacies, in most cases the brands will be different to those from home and usage instructions will usually be in Japanese only. It's a good idea to bring a few basic medications with you just in case. If you are traveling with a pre-existing condition you should bring enough of any prescription medicine you need for the duration of your stay and also carry copies of any prescriptions in case you need to get hold of some more. It's also a good idea to carry proof of medical insurance, and a note of your blood type and any allergies you have.

If you need to visit a doctor during your trip, most major hotels have access to on-call medical services and others will be able to direct you to a nearby hospital or clinic. There are also several **emergency and non-emergency help lines** offering English-language services that

Walking Tours

Although they aren't always cheap, tours lead by a good guide can bring Kyoto and Nara's histories and traditions to life. The cities certainly have no shortage of tour operators—be they volunteer guides who help out at a single temple or companies with a huge roster of professional guides. Pop into the tourist information centers in Kyoto and Nara (page 92) and the staff will be able to connect you to recommended guides and operators. On top of that, here are a few options we recommend.

Inside Kyoto (www.insidekyoto.com/kyoto-walking-tours): guided by a Lonely Planet writer and long-term Kyoto resident, the five walking tours on offer cost ¥20,000 to ¥25,000 (per group of up to 6 people) and take two to four hours in areas that include Arashiyama, Gion at night, and Fushimi Inari Shrine.

Cool Kyoto (http://cool-kyoto.net): Led by "last samurai" Joe Okada, a sword expert whose appeared on Letterman and has been guiding for over 50 years, this 5-hour Saturday tour takes in temples, shops, a sword demonstration, and more. Five to 30 people. ¥4,000/person.

Nara Walk (www.narawalk.com): As well as a "classic Nara" half-day walking tour (¥3,000/person) that takes in central Nara's main sights, Nara Walk has several other set tours in and around Nara and can also organize private, customized tours in Nara, Kyoto and Osaka (up to 9 people, from ¥17,000 to ¥32,000 per group).

can help locate medical care and provide interpretation where necessary (see Useful Telephone Numbers on page 92). All emergency service phone lines can handle English-language calls, although you may have to be put on hold before being put through to an English speaker.

Japan has relatively **low crime rates** and incidents of personal robbery or violence are low, but it is still necessary to take the same basic precautions for personal safety as you would in your home country. Cases such as the murders of Lucie Blackman in Tokyo in 2000 and Lindsay Hawker in 2007 are tragic reminders to be wary no matter how safe Japan's reputation is.

One notable danger in Japan is **earthquakes**. The country experiences thousands of mostly unfelt tremors annually. While the chances of your visit coinciding with a big quake are slim, it's still worth becoming familiar with escape routes at your hotel and evacuation zones nearby. If **a major earthquake hits, here's what you can do**. Stay away from windows as the glass can splinter, and, if you can, draw the curtains or blinds. If you are inside, stay there, taking cover under something sturdy such as a table. If you have time before taking cover, open any nearby doors to prevent them from jamming and blocking your way out later. If you are outside, go to the nearest open space, such as a park, where you'll be safe from falling objects. In coastal areas get to high ground as soon as the shaking subsides and stay there—more than 90% of the 18,000 deaths from the March 11, 2011 earthquake were attributed to the subsequent tsunami. As soon as possible after the quake, contact your embassy. The local TV channel NHK is the best source of immediate information when an earthquake hits, and English is available on some broadcasts. Information will also be posted online at the company's website: www.nhk.or.jp.

The **summer heat and humidity** can also be dangerous, especially if you are going from temple to temple, where you won't find much in the way of air-conditioning or respite from the heat. Keep well hydrated in summer, slap on sunscreen and a hat, avoid overdoing the sightseeing, and take other precautions against **heatstroke**. It sends more than 50,000 people to hospital every summer in Japan.

Internet and WiFi

Most Western-style hotels offer free in-room WiFi or broadband access, or at least will have a terminal or computer in the lobby available free to guests. Those that don't provide free access usually offer a paid service for a daily fee of around ¥1,000. It's less likely to find in-room Internet access in traditional accommodation like a *ryokan*, although some (such as Shunkoin Temple, page 58) will have in-room WiFi or a shared terminal or computer available to guests.

Besides the above, here are some places where you will be able to go online:
Kyoto Station Tourist Information Center (page 92). Along with free WiFi access, there are PCs available at ¥100 per 15 mins. Open daily 8.30 a.m.–7 p.m. On the second floor of Kyoto Station.
Kyoto International Community House (page 92). Near Keage Station (T09) on the Tozai subway line. PCs available at ¥200 per 30 mins. Open Tuesday to Sunday 9 a.m.–9 p.m.

Money Matters

The currency of Japan is the yen. The universal symbol is ¥, but sometimes it will be written in the original Japanese, 円, pronounced *en*. Bank notes come in denominations of ¥1,000, ¥2,000 (although you don't see these very often), ¥5,000, and ¥10,000. Coins come in ¥1, ¥5 (the only one without Western

numerals, but recognizable because of the hole in its center), ¥10, ¥50 (also with a hole), ¥100, and ¥500.

Japan is still predominantly a cash society, but credit cards are becoming increasingly accepted. Amex, JCB, Visa and Master Card are now widely accepted in hotels, restaurants, bars, taxis, and department stores in Kyoto, but always check beforehand—the safest approach is to assume you'll have to use cash and carry enough just in case.

ATMs at post offices and some convenient stores will also accept foreign-issued cards, including those using Amex, Cirrus, Maestro, Master Card, Plus, and Visa. Many bank ATMs will display signs saying they accept Master Card and the like, but whether or not they take foreign cards is very hit and miss.

Opening Hours

Although many office workers often start earlier than scheduled and remain in their offices well after 5 p.m., most business officially open Monday to Friday 9 a.m.–5 or 6 p.m. **Post offices** tend to open on a 9 a.m.–5 p.m., Monday to Friday schedule for most services (though the ATMs often open longer), with main branches also operating on shorter hours on weekends. **Banks** are only open on weekdays from 9 a.m.–3 p.m., although bank ATMs usually remain open until at least 8 p.m., with those in convenience stores open 24/7 year round. **Department stores** and other bigger shops typically open daily from 10 a.m.–7 or 8 p.m. **Museums** typically close on Mondays (or the following day if Monday falls on a national holiday), but remain open on weekends and national holidays, generally from 9 a.m.–5 p.m. **Doctors' and dentist's** offices tend to open in the morning, then close for lunch before opening again in the mid afternoon: a typical schedule being 10 a.m.–1 p.m.

and 3.30 p.m.–7 p.m. With all opening times, remember that banks, government offices, post offices, some tourist offices and many companies close on national holidays, during O-bon, and especially during the New Year holiday.

Useful Japanese

With three different sets of characters (2,136 Chinese *kanji* characters for regular use, and the 48 *hiragana* and 48 *katakana* characters) Japanese at first glance appears to be a very difficult language to grasp. Learning to read and write Japanese can indeed take many years. However, given the limited number of vowels and the fixed nature of their pronunciation, it isn't difficult to learn a few useful phrases for your trip.

A BRIEF GUIDE TO PRONUNCIATION

Throughout this book, when referring to place names or Japanese terms, such as Tokyo or Shogun (correctly Toukyou and Shougun), the long vowel has been omitted. In the section that follows, however, long vowels are indicated to give the correct native pronunciation.

Consonants are basically pronounced similarly to English, with the exception that g is always a hard sound (as in get). Vowel sounds work differently, as follows.

a as in c**a**t
e as in r**e**d
i as in ton**i**
o as in h**o**t
u as in p**u**t
ae is two sounds: a (as in c**a**t) and e (as in r**e**d)
ai as in Th**ai**land
ei as in sl**ei**gh
ie is two sounds: i (as in ton**i**) and eh
ue is two sounds: ooh and eh

BASIC PHRASES

Good morning **Ohayo gozaimasu**

Hello **Konnichiwa**
Good evening **Konbanwa**
Good night **Oyasumi nasai**
Goodbye **Sayonara**
My name is Smith **Smith (sumisu) to moshimasu (polite)**
It's nice to meet you **Hajimemashite**
Yes **Hai**
No **Iie**
Please **Onegai shimasu**
Please (offering something) **Douzo**
You're welcome **Dou itashimashite**
Thank you **Doumo (casual)/arigato or arigatou gozaimasu (standard)/ doumo arigatou gozaimasu (formal)**
I understand **Wakarimashita**
I don't understand **Wakarimasen**
Excuse me/pardon **Sumimasen**
Do you speak English? **Eigo wa dekimasu ka?**
How do you say it in Japanese? **Nihongo de nante iimasuka?**
What is this called? **Kore wa nan to iimasuka?**

HEALTH

Hospital **Byouin**
Doctor **Isha**
Dentist **Haisha**
Pharmacy **Yakkyoku**
Medicine **Kusuri**
Fever **Netsu**
Diarrhea **Geri**
Pain **Itami**
Cough **Seki**
Nausea **Hakike ga suru**
I have a headache/stomachache **Atama/ Onaka ga itai**
I'm ill **Byouki desu**
I have a cold **Kaze ga hikimashita**
I have the flu **Infuruenza desu**
Food poisoning **Shoko chuudoku**
I'm allergic to (nuts) **(nattsuu) arerugi desu**
Painkillers **Chin tsuyaku**
Stomach medicine **Igusuri**
Antiseptic **Shoudoku**

Antibiotics *Kosei busshitsu*

DIRECTIONS

(Excuse me,) where is the toilet?
(Sumimasen,) toire wa doko desu ka?
(Excuse me,) is there a bank near here?
(Sumimasen,) chikaku ni ginkou wa arimasu ka?
Straight ahead *Masugu*
On the left *Hidari ni*
the right *Migi ni*
Police box *Kouban*
Bank *Ginkou*
Department store *Depaato*
Supermarket *Supaa*
Convenience store *Conbini*

TRANSPORTATION

Train station *Eki*
Train *Densha*
Subway *Chikatetsu*
Bus *Basu*
Bus stop *Basu tei*
Airport *Kuukou*
Bicycle *Jitensha*
Ticket *Kippu*
Ticket office *Kippu uriba*
One-way *Katamichi*
Return *Oufuku*
Non-smoking seat *Kinen seki*
I want to go to (Arashiyama)
(Arashiyama) e ikitai no desu ga
Reserved seat *Shitei seki*
Non-reserved seat *Jiyuu seki*

WINING AND DINING

Do you have an English menu? *Eigo no menyuu ga arimasu ka?*
I would like (some water) *(mizu) o onegai shimasu*
Could I have the bill, please *O-kaikei o onegai shimasu?*
Thank you for the meal (said to staff when leaving a restaurant or to people at your table when finishing your meal)
Gochisosama deshita

SHOPPING

How much is (this)? *(kore) wa ikura desu ka?*
Do you accept credit cards? *Kurejitto kaado wa tsukaemasu ka?*
Cash *Genkin*
It's too expensive *Taka sugimasu*
I'll take this *Kore o kudasai*
Do you have…? …*wa arimasu ka?*

NUMBERS

Counting in Japanese can be challenging. Different systems are used for counting 1 through 10 for different things, and numbers are used in combination with a mind boggling array of qualifiers. From 11 onwards (thankfully!) there is basically a single set of numbers, though the qualifiers remain equally confusing.

ONE TO TEN FOR OBJECTS

1 *Hitotsu*
2 *Futatsu*
3 *Mittsu*
4 *Yottsu*
5 *Itsutsu*
6 *Muttsu*
7 *Nanatsu*
8 *Yattsu*
9 *Kokonotsu*
10 *Tou*
Example: I'd like two beers, please *Biiru o futatsu kudasai.*

COMMON NUMBERS FOR TIME, QUANTITIES AND MEASUREMENTS

1 *Ichi*
2 *Ni*
3 *San*
4 *Yon* or *Shi*
5 *Go*
6 *Rokku*
7 *Shichi* or *Nana*
8 *Hachi*
9 *Kyuu* or *Ku*
10 *Juu*

11 to 19 *Juu-ichi, Juu-ni, Juu-san*, etc
20 *Nijuu*
21 to 29 *Nijuu-ichi, Nijuu-ni, Nijuu-san...*
30 *Sanjuu*
40 *Yonjuu*
50 *Gojuu*
100 *Hyaku*
1,000 *Sen*
10,000 *Ichi-man*
100,000 *Juu-man*

MONEY

Bank *Ginkou*
Foreign exchange *Gaikoku kawase*
100 yen *Hyaku en*
1,000 yen *Sen en*
10,000 yen *Ichi-man en*
100,000 yen *Juu-man en*

Mobile Phones

You might find that you can use your own mobile phone in Japan if it has a roaming function and can work on Japan's 3G or 4G networks. However, you are most likely going to have to rent a mobile, if you want one for making calls. It's best to do so upon arrival at the airport, as there will be English-speaking staff available to talk you through the rates and rental packages available. KIX, Itami, Narita and Haneda airports have phone rental booths.

Useful Telephone Numbers

Police emergency: 110
Fire and Ambulance: 119
The AMDA International Medical Information Center (emergency and non-emergency medical assistance for non-Japanese speakers): 03-5285-8088
Japan Help Line (Toll-free, 24-hour, multi-lingual emergency assistance service): 0120-461-997/www.jhelp.com.
NTT telephone directory service: 03-5295-1010

Time

The whole of Japan operates in a single time zone, which is nine hours ahead of Greenwich Mean Time, 14 hours ahead of Eastern Standard Time and 17 hours ahead of Pacific Standard Time. Japan doesn't observe daylight saving time.

Tourist Offices and Websites

KYOTO STATION TOURIST INFORMATION CENTER

2nd fl., Kyoto Station Bldg. Tel. 075-343-0548. Open daily 8.30 a.m.–7 p.m.
The main tourist info center in Kyoto has staff who can speak English, Chinese and Korean, as well as loads of useful multi-lingual pamphlets and brochures about Kyoto and areas nearby. The staff here can help with hotel bookings and, along with free WiFi, there are PCs available for accessing the Internet (15 mins, ¥100).

KYOTO INTERNATIONAL COMMUNITY HOUSE

Open from 9 a.m.–9 p.m. Closed on Mondays. www.kcif.or.jp/en.
Designed more for foreign residents of Kyoto than visitors, there is a wealth of info to be found here, from a well-stocked library to notice boards about work opportunities and cultural events. It's worth stopping by to pick up free copies of their *Easy Living in Kyoto* guide and *Guide to Kyoto* map. There are also PCs available, if you need to get online (30 mins, ¥200). A 5-minute walk from Keage Station (T09) the Tozai subway line.

NARA CITY SIGHTSEEING INFORMATION CENTER

Kintetsu Nara Station
1st fl, Kintetsu Bldg, 28 Higashimuki Nakamachi, Nara-shi, Nara. Tel. 0742-24-4858. narashikanko.or.jp/en. Open daily from 9 a.m.–9 p.m.
Although the staff here speak only a little English, there are plenty of brochures available in English on the area's main sights and attractions.

KANSAI INTERNATIONAL AIRPORT

1st fl, International Arrivals Hall
Tel. 072-456-6025. Open daily from 8.30
a.m.–8.30 p.m. from Apr. to Oct. and from
9 a.m.–9 p.m. from Nov. to Mar. If you are
arriving through Kansai International
Airport (KIX) in Osaka, the airport's
tourism information center stocks
English-language brochures on Kyoto and
the rest of the Kansai area. Staff here
also speak English and there is free WiFi
on site.

Traveling with Kids

For many kids a day spent exploring Zen
gardens and ancient temples is about as
enticing as a bowl of boiled cabbage for
breakfast. As a nice balance to the cultural sights, Kyoto has a good range of
kid-centered attractions, such as the
Umekoji Steam Locomotive Museum, a
manga museum, and the samurai- and
ninja-fest that is TOEI Studio Park (see
page 74 for Kyoto's kid-friendly attractions). You could even do a day trip to
Universal Studios Japan (page 75) in
Osaka. Around town, you will also find
quite a few parks and open spaces where
kids can burn off some energy, be that
the Kyoto Imperial Palace Park (page 33),
Maruyama-koen by Yasaka Shrine (page
27) or even having a paddle in the Kamogawa River (page 35).

If you are traveling with children
young enough for **push chairs**, it's a
good idea to travel with a chair that is
light and easy to fold away (especially if
you want to get the most out of Kyoto's
excellent bus network). Also bring a suf-
ficient supply of **diapers**, **baby food** or
any other essential items, as although
Japan has all the items you will need,
you'll likely struggle to find familiar
brands or anything with English-
language packaging. **Breastfeeding** in
public isn't a taboo, but most women tend

to avoid it or do so discreetly. Department
stores always have private breastfeeding
rooms and a place for **changing diapers**,
as do some public buildings.

On **buses**, **trains** and **subways**, children under 6 get to travel free, while kids
aged 6 to 11 travel half fare. Places such
as **museums** and **amusement parks**
usually offer discounted admission to
children, which can be up to a 50% saving.
When booking a **hotel**, it's worth remem-
bering that Western-style rooms that can
accommodate more than three people are
scarce. Some of the bigger (and more
expensive) international chains will have
large rooms available, but otherwise
Japanese-style *ryokan* or *machiya* houses
(page 56) are a great option.

Visas

Citizens of Australia, Canada, Ireland,
New Zealand, the UK, the US, and certain
other countries can enter Japan for up to
90 days (if they are visiting for business
or vacation) without needing to get a visa
in advance. You'll be given a temporary
visitor visa upon arrival. Citizens of
Ireland, Mexico, Switzerland, and the UK
can then extend this visa for an additional 90 days while in Japan, while citizens of other countries will need to leave
Japan and then re-enter to do the same.

To enter Japan as a temporary visitor
you must be in possession of a passport
that will remain valid for the full duration
of your stay. By law you will also need to
have an ongoing ticket (or proof of one),
although this is not checked in most
cases. Upon entry you will also have to
have your fingerprints and photograph
taken.

If you are a citizen of a country not
mentioned above, you may need to arrange
your visa in advance. For more information
check the website of Japan's Ministry of
Foreign Affairs: www.mofa.go.jp.

INDEX

PHOTO CREDITS

About Tuttle: "Books to Span the East and West"

Our core mission at Tuttle Publishing is to create books which bring people together one page at a time. Tuttle was founded in 1832 in the small New England town of Rutland, Vermont (USA). Our fundamental values remain as strong today as they were then to publish best-in-class books informing the English-speaking world about the countries and peoples of Asia. The world has become a smaller place today and Asia's economic, cultural and political influence has expanded, yet the need for meaningful dialogue and information about this diverse region has never been greater. Since 1948, Tuttle has been a leader in publishing books on the cultures, arts, cuisines, languages and literatures of Asia. Our authors and photographers have won numerous awards and Tuttle has published thousands of books on subjects ranging from martial arts to paper crafts. We welcome you to explore the wealth of information available on Asia at **www.tuttlepublishing.com**.

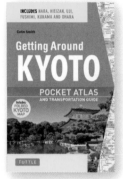
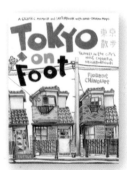

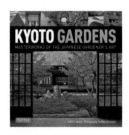
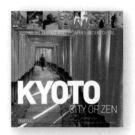